About Acting ⏤

About Acting ~~~

(with a bit of name-dropping
and a few Golden Rules)

~~~ PETER BARKWORTH

Secker & Warburg
London

First published in England 1980 by
Martin Secker & Warburg Limited
54 Poland Street, London W1V 3DF
Reprinted 1980
Reprinted 1981
Copyright © Peter Barkworth 1980

SBN: 436 03290 2

Typeset by Computacomp (UK) Ltd.
Fort William, Scotland
Printed in Great Britain by
Fletcher & Son Ltd, Norwich

To all my friends and colleagues mentioned in this book, without whose warmth and generosity I could not have written it.

Preface ⌒

Ask any actor who went to RADA in the late fifties and early sixties to name the teacher who influenced him most, and he is quite likely to answer very smartly on the cue: "Why—Peter Barkworth, of course!" Since then, the author of this book has become unique among those stars whose names above a title can guarantee success; he is the only one to have written a book with the avowed purpose of helping other and younger performers to do their job better.

Barkworth's position in his profession does not depend on chance gifts of voice or personality. It stands firmly on other attributes, among which are a natural feeling for style, a compendious and accurate emotional memory, a self-discipline which is almost monastic and a capacity for detailed observation which is balanced equally by a fund of sympathetic understanding of other people. One always feels with this actor that behind his work is the commitment of an entire self, that, figuratively, he never acts with his hands in his pockets, though he will do so physically if the needs of the part insist on it.

Inevitably, then, *About Acting* is a zestful book for actors—young, old, middle-aged; students, would-be students, amateurs even, bad actors even, in fact for anybody who knows that, come what may, he or she must somehow, somewhere, sometime, face an audience in a play, or else just die. All the above are recommended to absorb a dozen or two pages at bed-time and to repeat the dose till the book is finished, after which it should be kept very near the bed for constant reference. All the above will be the better for it, and not least those old hands who find in it advice that they received (or gave) years ago but in any case have now forgotten all about. They will be relieved too to discover that it is not a textbook on acting technique but something more rare and far more welcome: just the thoughts of a distinguished actor on how to deal with the problems that beset him and his colleagues in the practice of their craft.

For the acting student, in particular, the book bristles with relevance. Barkworth on the connection between speech and movement, on how to avoid being glib when you know all the lines backwards, on what he liked most about another actor's performance of Claudius in *Hamlet* (and, importantly, *why*), on how to cope with bad dialogue, and on the subject of concentration—it's all there. The corollary, that all performers, whether they are distinguished or not, or beginners or not, have the same difficulties to solve, will come as balm to anybody with a hard three years' slog at a drama school ahead of him.

Most important of all, this book is about excellence, although the author does not actually say so. That is why its most grateful readers will be the actors and actresses who have learnt their jobs, but who, during their long spells of unemployment, or burial in an unchallenging if lucrative television series, are beginning to wonder if the very idea of excellence has any point in relation to themselves. These are tempted to feel they are lucky if they work at all, and that to think about whether they can do it well enough is secondary to such questions as whether they ought to change their agent, how to be in the right place at the right time to land a job, and whether to snatch at a single exciting part in a provincial theatre or to find security in a soap-opera instead.

It is not easy for the talented minority to keep their sights on never, never doing less than their best. They will take heart from this book. To read it is an invigorating experience, confirming the true artist's conviction that to pursue excellence is as natural and as necessary as breathing.

John Fernald

Introduction ⌁

This book came about like this:

I started teaching at RADA in 1955. I had never intended to be a teacher and it seemed a bit pretentious to take classes there when I was a novice of twenty-six and when some of the students were considerably older than I was. But I had become depressed: I was playing small supporting roles in successful plays like *The Dark Is Light Enough* at the Aldwych Theatre, and *My Three Angels* and *South Sea Bubble* at the Lyric Theatre, and was getting little satisfaction from all that repetition, night after night, and felt that my talent, for what it was, was deteriorating and my confidence was in danger of disappearing altogether.

For a while I thought seriously, but rather romantically I suppose, of giving up the whole business and going off to some far-away place, like central Africa, to do good in the world.

But then I thought, no, the thing is to do something else during the day which will take my mind off those grisly two-and-a-half hours in the theatre every evening and give me something new to be enthusiastic about. It wasn't just boredom that was bothering me, but an acute form of self-consciousness (the greatest hurdle of all for some actors), which made it harder and harder for me to perform well. I found it increasingly difficult, as a run went on, to look and feel natural and spontaneous: everything seemed too set, too patterned, and therefore lifeless. I had a great deal to learn, so, I thought, rather contrarily and boldly, why not teach? School hours would fit in well with theatre hours, except on the mid-week matinée day; and I remembered I had enjoyed my only previous experience of teaching when I was in the Army after the war, doing my compulsory National Service, and I had had to give some lectures on Pay. I thought this time I might be able to take classes in Speech and Voice Production, so I asked a friend of mine who taught at the Webber-Douglas Academy if she thought it would be a good idea for me to approach the Principal there and ask to take a class or two.

"No," she replied, rather too quickly. "You see, we don't do things like that at the Webber-D. We have our own bunch of students, you see, and take them for everything ... we direct their plays and do the voice-production and movement classes ourselves." (I believe things have changed since then, and I'm relieved to hear it.)

"Oh," I said, nonplussed, knowing that I would be incapable of such an awe-inspiring and responsible task, "that's that, then."

"Why don't you try RADA?" she said, making it sound like a huge step-down, "I believe they do things like that there."

Don't be ridiculous, I thought, as I put the telephone down. But emboldened by a friend who said, "Well, they can always say no," I wrote a brief letter to John Fernald, who was then Principal, saying that I thought I would like to teach "perhaps something to do with speech", and if he was not interested would he please not bother to reply, but if he was I would be happy to come in and talk to him about it.

To my surprise he replied by return and suggested an immediate appointment. I was very nervous as I was ushered into his office, which, in spite of the rattling traffic in Gower

Street outside, was strangely hushed, and grander than I had remembered (I had been a student at RADA in the late forties), with soft lighting from large table-lamps, and a bigger desk than I had ever seen. He seemed yards away from me as I looked at him across it from my low chair and I found it very difficult to concentrate, but certain sentences pierced my hazy brain: "We could do with some young actors on the staff ... I think the students would like it ... but I don't want you to teach diction."

"Oh," I said, disappointed, for there was nothing else I thought myself capable of teaching.

"We've already got Clifford Turner and Barry Smith, and they're very good. And Denys Blakelock does audition speeches and things. No, I know what I want you to do: Hugh Miller is leaving, and I would like you to take over from him. He teaches 'technique', you know."

"Yes, I know," I said. "He taught me, actually..."

"Well, he is quite enthusiastic about your taking over from him, and so am I."

So! He has already mentioned it to Hugh Miller! It's all buttoned up, I thought.

"Whow!" I said.

"I like your work," he said, and my nervousness completely disappeared, "and I'd like you to start next term." He beamed at me, no doubt seeing how pleased I was, and how surprised. I think he even chuckled. He had a delightful way of chuckling, heaving his shoulders about. He sat back, waiting for me to speak, peering at me over his glasses. I stared at his bow-tie.

"Er ... what shall I do? I mean is there anything ... I mean ... what shall I include?"

"Go away and think about it," he said, "and work out a course of eleven lessons: a term's work. Two hours a week per class; two classes. We'll start at four hours a week. Nineteen shillings an hour."

"Is there anything you'd like me to include?" I repeated, as I got up from my chair and made for the door.

"I leave it to you," he said ... and then, "Well, yes, one

thing: I've noticed the students tend to be awfully clumsy with props—cigarettes, drinks, fans, books, that sort of thing ... you could include something to do with that ... and comedy, that's important."

"Right!" I said, and whooped my way along Chenies Street as far as Goodge Street station. I thought of little else for the next three months and worked out a course of lectures and exercises. Occasionally actor friends would be less than encouraging: "Those who can, do; those who can't, teach," they would chant, reminding me that there was still a stigma against actors who taught. This had always puzzled me; why was it all right for musicians to teach at the leading Academies, for painters and sculptors to teach at the Royal College of Art and the Slade, but not for actors to teach at RADA or Central or LAMDA? I was determined to fight the stigma: now, I think, it has disappeared, and many more actors have found their way into the major drama schools, their careers not suffering because of it.

John Fernald approved of my course when I outlined it to him, and I started to take the classes which had been assigned to me: "I think it should be fourth-termers," he said. Occasionally he would come in for a while to see what I was up to, but on the whole he left me alone, and I was completely free to get on with what I wanted to do.

He was a remarkable man and a great Principal. He trusted his staff and loved his students, and his concern for and knowledge of every single one of them always astonished me. He was an innovator, too: he reduced the numbers in each class from a staggering and hopelessly unmanageable thirty, and sometimes even more, down to about a dozen. He introduced a much more personal relationship between staff and students, and inaugurated repeat performances of plays by students in their final year: for them the Academy became more like a repertory theatre than a school; John Fernald always wanted students to get the feel of a professional theatre while they were still there under his guidance.

After my first term as a teacher he asked me if I would

take third-termers as well. This meant I had to enlarge my course, which I was only too happy to do, for it allowed me to experiment with new methods and exercises. Later I took the second term as well, and occasional classes for Finals students; and by 1958 I was working there more or less full-time, which was fine, for I was then in the middle of a three-year run of *Roar like a Dove* at the Phoenix Theatre. In that play I had a nice, funny part, but I was on the stage for only fifteen minutes in the second act, so the combination of the two jobs was not too exhausting, especially as I lived nearby, in an attic flat in Bloomsbury.

The idea of a book came from John Fernald. "Can you write about your classes?" he said, out of the blue one day. "I know you use the lecture-exercise method—don't you think you could make a book of your lectures?"

"I'll try," I said.

And I did, and failed. I realised that a great proportion of my lectures was based on demonstration and needed a perpetual comeback from the students. When I tried to write it all down it seemed very academic and long-winded and boring, so I gave up.

"Well, couldn't you make a book of the exercises?" he persisted. I tried that too, but failed again, because if the exercise is a good one the teacher has merely to set it without anticipating the result (if he says what the result should be, he spoils the adventure of the exercise). That's all right in the classroom, for the result can be analysed and discussed afterwards, but it's no good in a book. Too much would be left in the air.

For example, one of my favourite exercises was called "Going Round in Circles". Here is how I used to set it: "Next week I shall want you to perform a speech you already know—don't bother to learn a new one—and your task is to say it to someone who is standing outside a circle you keep going round. The idea of the exercise is of course to motivate properly the continuous movement, to motivate the moves towards and away from the other person, to find ways of going on an arc round him, to experiment with walking

xiv

backwards and sideways, and if possible to disguise from us the fact that it is just an exercise and even, if possible, to enhance the speech because of the variety of attitudes the moves will dictate."

This, believe it or not, is a wonderful exercise, and can teach an enormous amount about the intricacies of movement, about fluidity and about making points, about footwork and head-turns. It was often wonderfully well performed by the students and interestingly discussed by them afterwards. There seemed no way of conveying in a book the sort of excitement of discovery such an exercise can induce.

So I dropped the idea, and in time I left RADA. I wanted a break from teaching, and anyway was starting to work more on television than in the theatre, which meant that I no longer had my day-times free. I took my last class there in 1963.

Years later I was in Michael Frayn's play *Donkeys' Years* at the Globe Theatre. At every performance I gave an eight-minute party in my dressing-room. All the actors, except Penelope Keith and Andrew Robertson, who had an eight-minute scene in the middle of Act 2, used to come in, in their dinner-jackets, and drink Perrier Water (occasionally mildly laced) and talk actor-talk: we would discuss how the play was going at that performance, and what the audience was like; we would give each other occasional notes (this was allowed only within the confines of the party!) and generally chew the fat about plays, actors, directors, critics, authors and impresarios. Occasionally, too, we would play round-robin games: one rather malicious one, which had to be answered truthfully, was: "What is the compliment you most like to receive (a) as an actor, and (b) as a person?" The answers were very revealing.

Another was: "What advice given by other people has most helped you and affected your acting?" And it was with that question that the idea for this book dawned.

I ought to write, I thought, a book of short pieces:

Helpful Hints, Golden Rules, some which I have learnt from other people and others I have thought out for myself. Some of them may be clichés, but a good cliché has usually earned its reputation from the sheer repetition of its truth and usefulness. And rules are good, for when you know them it can be so rewarding to break them. At least you know what you are doing.

Two very dissimilar books influenced me greatly when I was considering the form of this one: J. B. Priestley's *Delight*, a compilation of 114 short pieces about things which have delighted him, and a recipe book called *The Flavour of France* by the Chamberlains: in it there is a recipe per page, accompanied by a photograph of the town or village from whence it came.

So here are my few recipes. You won't like them all, for acting is a very personal business, as personal as eating. But I hope you will like some of them, for they were born out of swapping ideas with my fellow actors at my Perrier party. I was quite touched when I heard the other day that Paul Eddington and John Quentin, who played the same part after me, kept up the tradition. I wonder what they talked about!

Before rehearsals start ⌐

Get The Facts Right ◦—•

"… remember, for all time, that when you begin to study each role you should first gather all the materials that have any bearing on it, and supplement them with more and more imagination, until you have achieved such a similarity to life that it is easy to believe in what you are doing. In the beginning, forget about your feelings. When the inner conditions are prepared, and right, feelings will come to the surface of their own accord." Constantin Stanislavsky, *An Actor Prepares*.

This is my favourite quotation. If you are one of those people who underlines memorable passages in books, here there is not a phrase you could leave out. I used to like starting a class with it at RADA, occasionally putting huge stresses on certain key words, like "easy" and "right". It sums up exactly what an actor's first task should be: to go for the facts, to get them right, to dig for the details of past life and present attitudes and, where there are gaps in the author's information, to fill them "with more and more imagination" until the jigsaw is complete.

It is necessary to know the past life of a character

3

because the past determines the present and the future. I was introduced to the theory of Determinism when I was a student at RADA. T. S. Eliot was all the rage then and, along with Auden, he was the poet most frequently chosen by us for diction and voice exercises. How often we listened to each other booming out:

> "Time present and time past
> Are both perhaps present in time future,
> And time future contained in time past."

But we never got tired of "Four Quartets", partly because they were so fascinating to speak, but also because they were the encapsulation of the theory we were all so keen on. "You are the result," said one of our teachers, explaining it, "of everything you have been and thought and done and inherited. The present is not self-contained, nor is it in a vacuum. So every character you play should be the result of what that character has been and thought and done and inherited."

There is no substitute for detail. A vague, generalised picture is no substitute for specific facts and figures. I remember reading a review in *The Times* which included the following damning sentence: "The actors acted with that kind of breathless intensity which actors always employ when they do not know what it is they are being intense about."

In the beginning forget about your feelings. Get the facts right.

Springboards ∽

Starting work on a part always feels to me like preparing to dive into a swimming pool. However many times you've dived before, there's always an element of danger. You stand there, transfixed for a moment, nervous, knowing you've got to plunge, but wondering if you dare to. The pause seems endless. Then, suddenly, as though by surprise, you're in.

I always like it, when I'm at my desk reading silently through a play, when I come to a speech which forces me to read it aloud. Often that speech becomes a model for the eventual performance; it can constitute the plunge, and is all the better for being unconsidered.

I go for the tone of voice first. That is my springboard. Precise or slack? Breathy or full-toned? Standard English or some variant? Fast or slow? Gradually a tone seems right. And by daring to read aloud a little more and a little more, the part begins to come to life: I can hear him.

Several of my friends do it this way. But not all. Wendy Hiller, for example, starts with her feet. "Yes, I'd like to take this part," she said, over tea at the Ritz, talking to Michael Codron, Peter Dews and Royce Ryton about her forthcoming role of Queen Mary in *Crown Matrimonial*, "because I know what her feet will be like." And then she demonstrated, apparently (I was not there), a delicate out-turning of her feet, and padded about on the deep carpets of the hotel. "Yes," she said, straightening her back, satisfied, "those are her feet. Those feet are royal."

Intentions And Beats ⌒•

These are the two words from "The Method" which I find the most useful. In fact they are indispensable; but so much has been written about them elsewhere that I will confine myself to the shortest possible explanation of them.

As you read and read the play and your part in it you will discover that underlying the words you are to speak there is a reason for speaking them. Why do you say that, to that person, now? Is it to convince your son, for example, that he is old enough to leave home now, and that it would be good for him to do so? Then that's your Intention. Is it to let your wife know that you know she is being unfaithful? Then that's your Intention. As soon as your son agrees with you, as soon as your wife knows that you know, those Intentions will be over and others will take their place.

A Beat is the distance from the beginning of an Intention to its end: it is the acting equivalent of a paragraph.

Write Things Down ⌒

Whatever your starting point, whatever your method, your performance will be an amalgam of the ideas which occur to you. So you might as well develop the habit of writing them down: if you don't remember your good ideas there was no point in having them in the first place, and in the hurly-burly of rehearsals it is all too easy to forget some of the valuable things you first thought of.

Remarks about the character, ideas for the subtext, and anything to do with the shaping of speeches are the things I like to scribble in my script as they occur to me.

I use a mixture of musical and other notation for the shaping of speeches:

⌒   between sentences means "join them up".

| between sentences or words means "pause" or "a beat" (a more usual meaning of the word than that on the previous page).

⌐| between sentences or words means "a tick pause": a very brief one.

|| means "a longish pause".

∩   means "a complete stop".

>   means "pounce on to this new idea".

___ under words means "give them emphasis".

——— over words means "throw them away".

∩   is a generalised symbol for sadness.

∪   is an equally generalised one for happiness.

∪∪ means "laughing the while".

f   means "loudly".

ff means "very loudly".

p   means "quietly".

pp means "very quietly".

⋀   in the left hand margin (it can vary hugely in size, sometimes it's as big as the page) means "enlarge the pressure or volume or whatever" and

⋁   means "diminish it",

and a line right across the page indicates the end of one intention and the beginning of a new one.

Squiggles over words give, by their rising and falling, an indication of a preferred inflection, eg:

         ̃   —   —   ̃
"Well, I'm not sure …"

I wouldn't want to clutter up a whole script with these aides-memoire (for that's all they are), but if an inflection has been awkward to find it's worth having a record of it.

I know a lot of actors don't like to mark up their scripts this way because they like the words to be uncluttered; but I do like to, even though I often change my mind about how things should go. My script becomes an incomprehensible mess of markings and crossings-out, but at least I can see the stages I have gone through.

The Voice Of The Author ⟿

The voice of the author, the voice of the character, and you: these are the three basic ingredients of any successful performance.

And of the three the hardest for an actor to realise is the voice of the author. This is especially so when the author is distinguished, for the fact that he is distinguished probably means that he is stylised, and the actor's task is to absorb that style and make it part of his characterisation.

The difficulty with performing the work of a stylised writer is that it can so easily sound as if you are quoting him rather than conceiving the words yourself. Therefore, and I'm necessarily generalising here, if he is Shakespeare, part of your *characterisation* must be that you think poetically; you are a poet, you are not merely quoting one. If he is Shaw, part of your characterisation must be that you are a good talker, high-spirited and intellectually bright. If he is Christopher Fry, you have a mind packed with images; if Tom Stoppard, your mind is even more packed with jokes, intellectual niceties and a huge vocabulary. Ibsen, Chekhov, Simon Gray, Michael Frayn, Noël Coward, John Osborne, T. S. Eliot all have their very individual voices, demanding not stylised performances but natural ones which have absorbed their style.

Go For The Life Of The Part ⌒•

"Go for the life of the part," said Edith Evans, when she was talking to some drama students in a television programme.

I was in two plays of which she was the star—Christopher Fry's *The Dark Is Light Enough* and Enid Bagnold's *The Chinese Prime Minister*—and I learned more from her than from anybody I have ever met. I want to include many of her Golden Rules in this book, and here is the first, for it complements what I've just been saying about an author's style. "*You* mustn't be stylised," she said, and she started talking about how to use a fan. "Those eighteenth-century ladies didn't use their fans for *style*, they *used* them. They would fan themselves if they were hot, or embarrassed, or poke somebody in the ribs with them if they wanted to make a point, or slap somebody on the shoulders with them if they were cross.

"You must go for the truth of a part, and know how the ladies and gentlemen of those times dealt with their clothes and wigs and make-up and accoutrements. Don't be stylised: be truthful!"

The Voice Of The Character ⌣⸱

I have at home a book called *A Book of Make-up* by Eric Ward, originally published in 1930. Nowadays it makes very strange reading. The idea behind it is that your own face should be obliterated by Leichner No. 5 and a new face, the face of the character, should be painted on. How things have changed! Nowadays actors wear hardly any make-up, and use it only to alter something in their own face which needs altering for the part.

So it is with characterisation. There is no question of obliterating yourself and starting a characterisation from scratch. Mostly you use yourself, and change only what is necessary. "Accept what is the same, and alter what is different," said Fabia Drake, one of my teachers at RADA, and that's it.

Find out what the differences are (age? accent? background? speech patterns? vocabulary? period? job? intelligence? instincts?) and exaggerate them for a while, to make sure they plunge themselves into your personality. Then you can forget about them; they will take care of themselves, and you can concentrate again on being yourself.

You ∼

Whether you intend it or not, what the audience will be most aware of in your performance is you: your appearance, your idiosyncrasies, your persona. However accurate your characterisation, the you-ness of you will dominate it. If you don't believe me, think of, say, twenty of your favourite performers. Think how their own personalities shine through all their performances. This is true even of actors for whom characterisation is of paramount importance: Laurence Olivier, Judi Dench, Alec Guinness, Alan Howard.

Your private life, therefore, spills over into your acting. It is bound to. Your qualities and your attitudes will all be in evidence, your personality will be on show. What you are in everyday life will be what you are in plays.

So a lot of your early work as an actor will be on yourself, developing your strengths, eradicating your weaknesses; and this not only in the big things but in the little things as well.

If you don't speak clearly in everyday life, you won't speak clearly in plays.

If you don't speak naturally in everyday life, you won't speak naturally in plays.

If you've got a funny walk in everyday life, you will have a funny walk in plays.

Stanislavsky again: "Never lose yourself on the stage. Always act in your own person, as an artist. You can never get away from yourself... Always and for ever, when you are on the stage, you must play yourself. But it will be an infinite variety of combinations of objectives and given circumstances which you have prepared for the part, and which have been smelted in the furnace of your emotion memory."

Memory ⏤

After talent (and what is that? oh! A desire to show off? I don't know. That's where it starts, I suppose: a desire to get up and show off in front of people. Then it changes), after that, the most important single attribute for an actor is a good memory. And I don't mean a memory for lines, but a memory for events, emotions: a storehouse of experiences. If knowing the differences between yourself and the character is the right approach to characterisation, an acute knowledge of yourself is pre-supposed, and you can get to know yourself only by remembering what you have done and what you felt like when you were doing it. You will have done a vast variety of things, and have experienced emotions from ecstasy to despair. What a pity to waste such a storehouse of experience by not using it in your acting!

Look ~

But your memory should be trained not only on yourself but on the people you meet and see around you. Looking, staring even, will fill you with knowledge of human behaviour, from deep revelations of loneliness, love, illness and age to the trivia of everyday existence: how people use their hands, their faces, how they walk and talk in shops, in church, in the street. Tourists are very interesting to watch, absorbed as they are in the foreign-ness of everything around them, trying to find their exact location on a yellow and green map provided by the hotel, or in their *A to Z.* Being a tourist is as near as an adult can become to being a child again, with a mind uncluttered with the paraphernalia of sophistication and getting-on-with-people; there is a simple, straightforward concentration on looking, a concentration actors could well attempt to emulate.

Models ⸺

So the world around you will fill you with ideas which, hopefully, will become deep-seated in your memory.

Sometimes, however, it is good to seek a more specific model for a part. I like to do this. I remember when I was preparing for *Professional Foul* by Tom Stoppard, in which I had the part of a Professor of Ethics at Cambridge University, I watched Professor A. J. Ayer on television deliberately to spy out some of his mannerisms and idiosyncrasies. I noticed, for instance, that his words had great difficulty in keeping up with his racing intellect, so he would rush the last words of one sentence because the next one had formed in his mind. I liked, too, his habit of delaying laughter at one of his own jokes: he would crack a joke, then say another sentence, then laugh at his joke during the sentence after that. I liked his mercurial changes of mood, violent changes really, revealing themselves so quickly in his face as the thoughts flashed by. I liked the actual speed with which he spoke. All good stuff. All grist to the mill. Many television performers, rightly chosen, from Kenneth Clark to Magnus Pyke, can give a picture of some aspect of a part one is playing.

Get The Job Right ⤙•

Are you a soldier, a dustman, a doctor, a lawyer, a king, a Prime Minister, a housewife, a cook, a marriage guidance counsellor, a televison producer, a teacher, a nurse, a company director, a mother? Get the job right, and that's half the battle. It was Clifford Evans who pointed this out to me, and I've always been grateful to him.

At the moment of writing, there is a beautiful play by Brian Clark called *Whose Life Is It Anyway?* at the Savoy Theatre, and one of the glories of Michael Lindsay-Hogg's direction is that you really believe you are in the presence of doctors and nurses and psychiatrists and lawyers, and not in the presence of actors. It is the result of painstaking observation of the details of each profession: nurses and doctors have a way of walking through wards and along corridors which is not the way you and I walk along them; doctors have a vocational caring for their patients, and carry more in their heads than they intend to reveal. They have special sorts of hands, too, sensitive, careful, instructive.

The difficulties about playing the public figures who so dominate Shakespeare's plays have always fascinated me, for the actors have the double task of finding the true public face

19

of these characters, and the true private face as well. I have never yet seen a Claudius, for example, who has managed to achieve this duality. In his first scene he is in public, a new king, worried, obviously, by Hamlet's sulky withdrawal but nevertheless, surely, putting on as brave and impressive a public face as possible. The scene can be played with smiling, royal politeness, with its demands for compliance from Hamlet disguised as soft entreaties; but so often the actor chooses to rant and rage, making the task of the poor performers playing Gertrude, and all the courtiers, very difficult indeed! How to react? Certainly their first task will have to be to depose this madman, totally unfitted as he is to occupy Denmark's throne. And Claudius has plenty of scope, later in the play, for self-revelation: if all is revealed straight away, there are no surprises in store.

I did see one actor do the end of the play-scene magnificently. He pretended he thought the play had finished, rose and applauded. The rest of the (on-stage) audience joined in the clapping. And then, as though it were *nearly* an ordinary command, he turned to a courtier and said, "Give me some light. Away."

The underplaying of this superb theatrical moment, putting on the public face instead of the usual shouting and storming, doubled its impact.

Learn The Lines ⁓•

"Of course," you say. "What an imbecilic piece this is going to be! Of course I shall learn the lines."

Ah, but I think by the time you've read it you may find it one of the hardest in the book to agree with, because the reason I am putting it so near the beginning, when I am concerned with the initial preparation for a part, is that I think it best to learn the lines before rehearsals start.

Or at least to have a pretty good idea of them. When Noël Coward directed his own plays he insisted that the cast arrive word-perfect for the first rehearsal. And the distinguished director Murray Macdonald often used to say to me: "I get so bored with actors who don't know the lines and struggle away with them at rehearsal that I sometimes want to give up directing altogether."

However, my reasons for believing that it is good to know the words before rehearsals start do not include placating directors! Indeed the one penalty you may incur is that your colleagues—director and cast alike—will resent your being ahead of them. But even this can eventually become an advantage, especially when time is short (as it always is for an episode in a television series, or even, now,

21

for a West End play: four weeks always used to be allowed for rehearsals, now it's three), for it encourages everyone else to get a move on. You may be accused, too, of being less receptive to other people's ideas, less influenced by the other actors, less sensitive to the nuances they are beginning to discover in their roles. I find the reverse to be the case. Actors who have no knowledge of the lines, who like to start from scratch, who bore everyone with endless arguments as to the meaning of the lines and the attitudes underpinning them, don't even notice what you are doing because they have their faces buried in their scripts. They don't react at all to you: they cannot. Whereas you, from the start, can look at them, speak to them, listen to them, be surprised by them (holding the script the while, of course: you won't want to throw it away right at the beginning); and this element of surprise, if you remember it, is one of the most valuable things that can happen. So often it is totally lacking, and plays become flat and bland because of the lack.

If you have learnt the lines in the leisure of pre-rehearsal days (if, as we say, you have done your homework), you will perforce have worked on their meaning and subtext. Indeed, you will have learnt them *by* working on their meaning, by reading them over and over again, until the words have gradually and unforcedly sunk into your subconscious. You will have fought over the difficult bits, and even have worked out suggestions for possible alterations. In short, you will come to rehearsals knowing what you are talking about; you will have some idea of how you want to play the part.

I have found that, if the director disagrees with elements of my homework, it is quite easy (providing the director is right, of course!) to change them. Directors are, on the whole, better at altering a positive contribution from an actor than at suggesting how a part should be played when the actor starts with nothing: I have seen disasters happen to actors who have allowed a director to tell them how to play a part.

The most important advantage, though, of having a good knowledge of the words in advance is that it enables

22

you to assess more clearly the rightness or wrongness of the moves a director may suggest. That is usually his first task, and where you stand or sit, or when you move about, is as much as anything going to determine your eventual performance. If you know the words you can *look*. You can sense the distance between you and the other actors, you can feel when a move is a good one. You may even suggest some good ones yourself.

Edith Evans liked to do this; when a distinguished director started giving her moves she said, "No, no, no! You mustn't tell me where to go, or when to sit! I must work that out for myself."

"But Dame Edith," wailed the director, "if I'm not to give you moves, what am I here for?"

"Oh," she said, "we'll find something for you to do."

I will bring this overlong piece to a sudden end with just one more observation. I think rehearsals should be fun. Work is all the better and all the quicker for a few laughs and a few jokes ... and jokes and laughs are possible only when people do not feel the oppressive weight of work on their heads. Learning the lines in advance takes the chore out of rehearsals, lightens the load, and therefore lightens the atmosphere.

You still don't agree with me? Oh well.

First rehearsals ~

Don't Throw Away The Read-Through ⌒

Meeting the cast and director for the first time can be a nerve-racking experience. Actually it is a comfort to know that all the other actors are just as nervous as you are, and the director is probably more nervous than anyone. And if you have done your homework you will not let your nerves wreck the day for you, but will use the read-through as it ought to be used: it is, after all, your first opportunity to talk and listen to the people you are going to be with in the play.

Robert Lewis, in my favourite book about acting, *Method or Madness?* (he plumps for the Method!), says: "Beginnings are extremely important ... the things you should do in your first reading (because it is exploratory work and you are trying to find out what goes on) are *talk* and *listen*."

Both activities will yield many surprises if you are really concentrating and, again, those surprises are worth remembering.

Talking ⌣

When you talk you are thinking of two things: what you are talking about, and the person, or persons, to whom you are talking. Sometimes what you say has most of your attention (if it's a memory, for example, or something which is difficult to think out or to find the right words for); sometimes the person you are addressing has (if you are telling him what to do, or asking for his sympathy or advice). It is one of the most interesting things to work out: where does the majority of your attention lie at any given moment?

But you talk for the benefit of other people, not for yourself. If they weren't there, you wouldn't talk. It is for them.

Obvious, and yet it is distressing to see—particularly in "speechy" plays by, say, Shakespeare and Shaw—how many performances are ruined by actors who forget they are actually talking *to* someone.

Listening ~

"Listening," said Edith Evans, "is paying attention. It is *not* reacting. I can't bear it when I'm talking to another actor on the stage and he *reacts* to everything I say. Listening is blank-faced usually... if it's gracious listening a smile is allowable. But listen! Don't react!"

I love that. It's true.

As is Flora Robson's dictum, in a speech she gave to RADA students, that "Listening is receiving. Talking is giving, listening is receiving."

Your Attitude To The Director—1

Continuing for a moment my theme of talking and listening (and doing one of those two things is how you will spend most of your time in most plays), I would like to tell you what my first television director, Lionel Harris, said to me: "Don't try to convince *me*, don't try to convince the *camera*: convince the people you are with. Convince them that you are really talking to them and really listening to them. Try to pretend I'm not here. When you're in the studio, try to pretend the camera is not there. You won't succeed, but the attempt is worthwhile!"

This really is a Golden Rule for acting in television; but I think it has enormous relevance to acting in the theatre as well. It is so tempting, there, to talk to the audience and to listen to them, instead of talking and listening to the other characters.

Your Attitude To The Director—2 ⌒

Lionel Harris also said: "I always say to my casts and, when I'm lecturing, to students at drama schools, that they should not take too much notice of what I say. You see, the actor is the one who has to do it, and do it night after night, and he must be comfortable. Clever actors will remember what they like about what I've told them and conveniently forget what they don't like, and I never reprimand them for it. So. Don't be too obedient!"

I had been immensely worried when I was being directed by John Gielgud in a revival of *The School for Scandal* at the Haymarket Theatre in 1962. I was Sir Benjamin Backbite, and I remember that just before the read-through he suddenly turned to me and said, "I think it would be amusing, Peter, if you said all your R's as W's. For example, let's see, yes, here, your third speech: instead of 'To say truth, ma'am, 'tis very vulgar to print', you should say, 'To say twooth, ma'am, 'tis vewy vulgar to pwint.'"

The rest of the cast laughed, but it threw me into consternation because, to say truth, I didn't think it was the best idea in the world; but I felt I couldn't start the rehearsals by having an argument with Sir John, whom I admired and liked so much—no one is kinder and more generous than he—so I let it go. I tried to do it straight away and of course made an utter mess of it and felt wretched and humiliated.

At later rehearsals he gave me an immense amount of business, including, I remember, trying to balance a small cane on my chin! This not while I was speaking but while Margaret Rutherford was. I could feel the rest of the cast didn't like it but, again, because it was John Gielgud, and I was in awe of him, there seemed nothing for it but to be obedient.

Eventually I confessed my worries to Meriel Forbes, who was playing Lady Sneerwell, and she said: "Darling, you mustn't be so obedient! John would be shocked if he knew you were so worried. What he is doing, darling, is offering you pearls. But you have to supply the string yourself, and any pearls which won't fit on to your string, you must discard."

But the W's remained, I'm afraid. By sheer repetition both good things and bad things stick; and the good things get better and the bad things get worse.

Your Attitude To The Director—3 ⌒

Television has brought about a much more democratic relationship between actors and directors, for a television director is a performer too, supervising the cameras' moves and the cuts from one camera to another. He is not just an onlooker.

This new democracy has permeated through to the theatre as well, and is to be applauded. It is up to actors to maintain it, and there is one area where I think we often fail to, and that is in the giving of praise.

Actors are known to thrive on praise. "Don't criticise me," Dame Edith implored Peter Brook, during a rehearsal of *The Dark Is Light Enough*, "praise me! What I want is praise!"

We all do. In our hearts we all do. We can take anything from a director who starts by saying: "It's coming along beautifully, your performance ... it gets better every day ... there's just one thing ..." As John Fernald says in his book *Sense of Direction*: "All actors incline towards insecurity some of the time, and the best of them much of the time; a director may well be judged by the rapidity with which he can dispel this inclination."

True; but what we are not good at is giving praise. To praise the director for his good and helpful ideas, the author for his skilful writing is, if it's truthful, nothing to do with sycophancy: it is to give encouragement and confidence in exactly the same measure as we would like to receive them.

Praise should be a two-way affair.

Your Attitude To The Cast 〜•

Take care to acknowledge that they have as many insecurities as you have, will probably prefer not to be watched too closely at early rehearsals when they are finding their way, and will be much happier to think that you are not sitting there criticising them, either silently or in whispers to someone else. We are all so damn' sensitive, that's the pity of it! I remember my confidence falling through the floor at an early rehearsal for a stage play when I caught sight of a girl exchanging a kind of deprecating grimace with another, while I was struggling away with a long speech. When confidence goes, boldness goes and daring goes, and boldness and daring are too valuable to be allowed to evaporate in early rehearsals. I like it when the rest of the cast seem not to be taking too much notice of what I am doing, when they read newspapers (as long as they don't rattle the pages), or do the crossword, or knit.

We are a critical lot, and I think it is better to curb criticism of your fellow performers as much as you can. If you criticise them you can bet your bottom dollar they will criticise you.

Do as you would be done by.

35

Concentration ◞

If your attitudes to the director and the cast are as kindly as I have recommended, you will more easily gain the enormous and necessary bonus of concentration; concentration is impossible in unfriendly surroundings.

To be able to concentrate easily, and ignore the many distractions in a rehearsal room, a theatre, or a film or television studio, is a knack which has to be acquired. And the place to acquire it is in everyday life.

Train yourself to listen well, to remember people's names as you are introduced, to remember, like a photographer, the look of people and places and things, and to see them in your mind's eye in colour.

Give yourself these exercises:

1. Concentrate, when alone, on a memory, without allowing distracting thoughts to invade and spoil it.
2. Work out arithmetical problems in your head, or argue, in your head, through a personal problem.
3. Read. (Have you noticed that people who read a lot, or write, are particularly good at concentrating?)

4.   Learn to talk well, so that there is a clear connection between what you are thinking and the words you use to express those thoughts. "Talking-practice" is what I call it, this exercise of talking alone over a wide range of subjects: half an hour of continuous chatter (your family will think you've gone mad), and the sentences will flow out of you, connecting your voice to your head.

Look. Listen. Read. Talk.

Moves ⌁

Sometimes called "Blocking", "Plotting", "Seeing What Happens", or—Barry Davis's favourites—"Busking", "Bluffing", or "Finding your feet".

I like it best when everybody pretends to be very casual about it. "OK," said Michael Lindsay-Hogg, one of our finest television directors (we were finding our feet in *Professional Foul*), "OK. So. There's this hotel room. I tell you what's already been decided and that's where the walls are because the scenery is now being made and so that tape on the floor indicates where the walls are and there are a couple of doors, one into the corridor, there, and one into the bathroom, there. So. There'll have to be a bed somewhere, and a chest-of-drawers like they have in Czech hotels, and a couple of chairs, I suppose. But they can be anywhere. The only thing is, of course, that when we've decided where we'd like them to be in *this* room, the other rooms—you know, for the reporters and footballers and all—will have to be sort of similar because they are in Czech hotels. So... Peter... er... well, look, just come in, eh? ... and... er... well, come in ... see what happens..."

This approach, which allows everyone to chip in and

feel their way through a scene, is very relaxing, and moves invented in a relaxed atmosphere need less amending at later rehearsals because they start from a premise that comfortableness is what counts. Not cosiness, comfortableness. Only when an actor is comfortable will his performance grow.

"OK then, Peter?... Stephen?... Looks good... feel OK? We'll come back to it tomorrow... but that's the groundwork ... OK?"

I can't bear being given arbitrary moves arbitrarily preconceived by the director. Only sleepless nights and awkward arguments ensue, for such a director discards one of the most precious ingredients in the making of a play: the actors' instincts.

Anchors ⌐

This and the next eleven pieces are just a few tips about blocking and moves and positions and things.

"I must have my anchors!" said Edith Evans when we were rehearsing *The Chinese Prime Minister*. When I asked her what they were she said: "Anchors are the people or things around you on the stage, onto which you can latch your thoughts. They are, quite simply, the people and things you look at. Where you *look* is extremely important."

She pointed out to me how they helped her in a particular scene. "I'm here, d'you see, and you're there. As I have the most to say, I'm sitting in the upstage chair. So you're down there. Sitting. And sitting still, I hope. Ah yes," she said, "you must be still when I am talking to you because I'm like a horse, d'you see: if you move about, I shy. Like a horse shies at a hurdle. Anyway. There you are down there, on my left. You are my left-hand anchor. I need something on the other side of me. I need a right-hand anchor. Now: there's nobody else on the stage, so it has to be a thing. I've made it this little table to the right of my chair. I shall drink during this scene, d'you see, and from time to time I shall put my glass down on this little table. If the table were on the

40

same side of me as you are it would be no use to me, because the importance of having anchors on both sides of me is that it enables me to *turn* from one to the other. This means that the audience sees much more of my face, and it also enables me to make points... you know that rather cross little line I have to you? Well, just before, I shall have taken a drink and put my glass down on the table, so that I can *turn* to you, suddenly, and make a point of my moment of crossness."

Anticipation ~

The example Dame Edith gave me of her use of anchors leads to the truism: "What you are doing now must be right for what you are doing now, and right for what you are going to do next."

I have forgotten which bit of the play she meant now, but her lines were something like: "Yes, he was a splendid man, your father. A pity you don't live up to him." Putting the glass down during the first sentence was good, for pictures of my father were in her mind and the audience could see them; and it was also good because it was right for what she did next, which was to turn to me suddenly for the second sentence, "that rather cross little line".

Talking Off ⌐

I learned this from a wonderful American actress called
Evelyn Varden, who was in Lesley Storm's play *Roar like a
Dove*. Unhappily she became very ill during the course of the
three-year run at the Phoenix Theatre, and died shortly after
her return home.

Here is an example of "talking off": you are looking
round a room and remarking on various ornaments and
pieces of furniture. Once you have seen an object you can
turn away from it *while talking about it*, so that your eye can
alight more readily on the next object to which you are
going to refer.

Evelyn's part was Muriel, an American matriarch,
visiting her daughter who was married to a Scottish Earl. On
her first entrance she looked around the library, inspecting
it. Her speech went:

"The lamps are new ... and those drapes ... (*she wanders
up to the yellow curtains, touches them*). Very nice ... but in
America we got over that yellow craze years ago ... (*She
glances at a small table*) Gracious—where's the snuff box that
belonged to Prince Charlie?"

Now. Having looked at the lamps, she turned "off"

them and looked towards the curtains while saying, "The lamps are new", so that she could say almost immediately, "and those drapes". She used the line, "but in America we got over that yellow craze years ago" to look towards the small table.

This device is very useful, for it is extremely natural, and it helps you to get a move on.

Aftersurge ⟶

"Do you play golf?" Edith Evans asked me one day, and went on, without waiting for a reply, "because if you did you would know what I mean by the follow-through. You hit the ball, d'you see, and then afterwards you lift the club high above your head like that, and hold it there. That's the follow-through. It's the same in a play, d'you see: you say a line, but the thought behind the line does not stop the moment you've said it: there's a follow-through."

(A nice Golden Rule from this is "Go on thinking about what you were thinking about until the next thought occurs to you.")

The aftersurge is a development of the follow-through. I learned the word from Hugh Miller. "The aftersurge of emotion" was how he described it, and he explained it like this: "When one of those enormous anti-aircraft guns, or those the Germans used to shoot at us from across the Channel, has been fired, it immediately recoils and then slowly resumes its firing position. Even a rifle does this. When you've fired, it jerks back at you for a moment. It can be quite a nasty surprise the first time you experience it. Well, when in a play you have powerful emotions to express,

45

the emotions do not stop at the ends of the lines. There is an aftersurge. This aftersurge is best expressed in a move. Aftersurges can provide some of the most effective moves in a play."

Then, without any warning, he turned on one of the students and said, really angrily: "Don't you ever behave like that again!"—and he turned slowly away, in deep anger, walking a step or two, and then turned back and said, even more viciously: "I've had just about as much from you as I can stand!"—and again he moved away, this time in another direction, occasionally looking at some of the rest of us, and we were all scared in case we were going to be the next recipient of this apparently unwarranted anger; a pause ensued, but his anger with the same student was inexorable, for he turned back again and shouted: "You have no right to upset the class in this way!" The poor student was distraught, wondering what on earth he had done to incur such displeasure, but still Hugh Miller, after another move away, turned back (by now he had travelled more or less round the room): "You don't *listen* to what I say, you criticise it, you argue with it; your stupid face gives you away!" By now the student had gone quite white, and Hugh Miller, like a stalking lion, went to the far end of the classroom. Then he pointed to the door and yelled: "Now get out! Get out! Get out!" And the student got up and left the room.

Hugh Miller rescued him. "Come back!" he said, all kindness and niceness, "Sit down!" Then he turned to the rest of us. "That's the aftersurge. It allows you to go anywhere, and it has the huge advantage of making moves away from people easier to perform; it helps you to break up your speeches: you noticed how I was able to walk away and then turn back, to walk away again and then turn back.

"Of course," he said, beaming at his poor victim, "the emotion doesn't have to be anger. But it's the easiest with which to demonstrate."

Footwork .—.

Anchors, Anticipation and the Aftersurge (the three "A's", I used to call them at RADA) are to my mind the most helpful of all technical devices, the most useful to know about.

They all rely for their effectiveness on really controlled footwork. "Watch my feet," said Hugh Miller, as he demonstrated the aftersurge again—we had been so mesmerised the first time that we hadn't really noticed what he was doing—"and you'll see how smooth, how slack, how relaxed they are, and how walking about on a stage does not always mean walking forwards: you can walk sideways, like a crab, or you can walk on an arc round a person, or even walk backwards."

Laurence Olivier said, when he was talking to me about technique in acting, that his two favourite commands to himself were: "Relax your feet!" and "Always have more breath than you need!"

Years later, I was in a production for television of Royce Ryton's play *Crown Matrimonial*, and Anna Cropper, who played the Princess Royal, was rehearsing a scene where she was walking along a corridor talking to a Lady-in-Waiting.

Anna was walking somewhat faster than the actress playing the Lady-in-Waiting, so in order to keep talking to her she suddenly turned and started walking backwards. Having stopped talking, she turned forwards again and walked into a room.

I was standing with the director, Alan Bridges, and he whispered to me: "There's an actress for you! She knows how to walk backwards."

New Move On A New Thought ·—·

A new thought can be a good springboard for a move, especially if the two things coincide, almost jerkily.

It is good to go through your part to find which of the things you say can be things which just occur to you. Comb through your part for new thoughts, and moves may well spring out of them, for new thoughts come with energy, and it is that energy which converts itself into a move.

Follow Your Thought ⌁

Put a look in the direction in which you are going before you go, and the move will look and feel more natural.

For example, you are sitting talking to someone. Over there, on the other side of you, is a table with drinks on it. Contrive while talking to look round at the drinks. Some time afterwards, go and get one.

Or, for example, you are in a bad mood, and you turn away from the person who is hurting you. Wherever you look when you turn away can establish the direction you take for your next move.

Or, look down before you sit; look up before you stand.

A bit bald, but it's not bad, and it works.

Practical Moves ⟋

Many moves can be made for emotional reasons, but it is easy for them to become clichés: how tired one becomes of the perpetual rise in anger, or sit in despair! "I think that would be a good moment for you to rise and walk round the back of the sofa," I can hear a director say, or, "I think that would be a good moment for you to sit."

One way to avoid such clichés is to give the move, if possible, a practical purpose as well: you rise not only because you are agitated but to look for an ashtray as well; you sit not only because you are feeling more relaxed but to tie up a shoe-lace as well. Etc. etc.

Suit The Action To The Word 〜

There was an electrifying sequence in Tom Stoppard's *Night and Day* at the Phoenix Theatre. Diana Rigg, as Ruth Carson, had just been told of the death of Jake Milne (played by Peter Machin), a young reporter she had just got to know and to whom she was attracted. When his death was announced she was standing with her back to the audience at a table with drinks on it. She put her glass down and clinked another one with it. A little later she walked, apparently calmly, across the stage and suddenly banged a pillar with her fist, and hugged it for a while. Her face gave nothing away, for her husband was there.

I can imagine—I do not know, for I haven't asked her— that those brilliantly chosen actions were an immense help, night after night, to the re-creation of the feelings induced by the news of the death of the boy.

It's a bit like praying, really. Why is it easier to pray if you kneel down, close your eyes and put your hands together? I don't know, but it is. The action reminds you of praying.

Thoughts inspire actions. Actions, rightly chosen, inspire thoughts. Suit the action to the thought.

Do Things At Different Speeds ⤙

This, again, is from Laurence Olivier, who pointed out the value of walking slowly if you are talking quickly, and walking quickly if you are talking slowly. "Much better," he said, "than the cliché of rushing about and talking quickly, or strolling and talking slowly."

Try it!

Use The Visual ✦

This is one of my favourites. It means refer, either by look or by gesture, to things which are outside the set in which you are acting. "He's upstairs," can be accompanied by a look or a gesture (however small) to the room upstairs. It makes "upstairs" more vivid, and therefore more believable. "No, he's not here, he's in Kent somewhere," can be accompanied by an albeit vaguer gesture in the direction of Kent—at least it places your room geographically, and even that helps believability.

Penelope Keith, as Lady Driver in *Donkeys' Years*, used the visual for a wonderfully comic moment. We were standing in an Oxbridge courtyard, and she was telling me that her husband Harry was "away this weekend".

"Oh, Harry's away, is he?" I said.

"He's in Montreal," she said, pointing vividly in the direction in which she assumed Montreal to be. The audience caught the ludicrousness of it, and hooted.

Using the visual can apply not only to looks and gestures but to moves as well. I had a line in a television play which referred to my garden outside and how proud I was of it. The director wanted me to go on sitting where I was, chatting to a visitor.

54

"Can't I get up and look out of the window?" I said.

"No," he said.

"Why not?" I said.

"Because actors aren't good at looking out of windows," he said.

What an odd thing to say, I thought. But then I thought, no, I know what he means: some actors forget that when they look out of windows they can see specific things in specific places; instead they give a generalised look in the direction of the generalised world outside.

"Why do you want to look out of the window?" he asked.

"Because it will make the garden more vivid. The audience can't see it, but if I look at it they'll believe it's there."

"Well, you won't get a close-up," he said, "because I can't get a camera outside the window."

"I don't mind," I said.

"Show me!" he said.

I showed him.

"All right," he said, "I see your point ... and ... yes ... that's good ... because it means you're nearer the door, so you'll be able to lead the way into the dining-room. Yes, that's good. And I'll give you a close-up in the dining-room!"

Turn Your Back ❧

"If you've got a long part," said Clive Brook, when I was acting with him in a revival of *A Woman of No Importance* at the Savoy Theatre in 1953, "spend some of the time on the stage with your back to the audience. It stops them getting bored with your face."

Homework ⌒·

Planny-Anny ⌁

Having plotted the play you will want to do another long session of homework: there are so many things to be chewed over away from rehearsal, in the relaxation and privacy of home. This is what I call my Planny-Anny stage. A silly phrase, but it's stuck with me now. Actors, unlike painters, writers and composers, have to do much of their creating in the company of colleagues, and however relaxed you try to be at early rehearsals there is always a certain tension, and it is good to reconsider the ideas you've had and the decisions you've made in more tranquil surroundings.

Often, during these homework sessions, new and delicious ideas will occur; and you can use them, too, for more precise work on those bits which seemed awkward at rehearsal. Do you need, for example, to work out what to do with your hands? Is putting them in your pockets for the entire scene good enough? Some actors don't need to work on their hands, others do. Every actor finds some things difficult; you may be ashamed to mention your particular difficulties to your colleagues, so home is the ideal place to solve the problems they induce.

Your imagination is freer to roam, and you may well

think of using props rather more than you had anticipated. "Yes," you might think, "I've got to go from my office to hers—why don't I take something with me, even if it's only a file, and plonk it on her table? That'll help that move."

The first rehearsals, and the Planny-Anny sessions which follow, are for working out what you are going to do. That, for me, is the part of acting which is the most fun.

After that it all gets a bit more serious!

Further Rehearsals ⟶

Attitudes ~

At this stage you will be deeply engrossed in yourself and your performance; you will be trying new ideas at rehearsals, and be testing the results of your recent homework.

To counteract all this self-absorption you must now start considering what your attitudes are to the other people, not as *actors* (I have dealt with that already) but as *characters* in the play. How do they affect you? Do you like them, are you in love with them? Do they make you shy, do they bring you out of your shell? Are you at ease in their company, are you suspicious of them? Do you hate them? If you do, how much are you prepared to reveal that hatred, how much do you keep it a secret?

If you are like me, you will, in everyday life, feel very differently in the company of different people. So it should be in your acting too. And yet it rarely is, is it? I mean, when you look at plays you get some idea of the characters, but you rarely sense that a character changes when his companions are different.

Especially should you know how much, and in what way, your attitude to each character *develops* as the play progresses.

63

Affections—mother-and-child, friends, lovers—are very differently expressed in everyday life, and should be in plays, too. C. S. Lewis is marvellously clear about affections in his book *The Four Loves*.

Cover-Ups ⌣

I'm shy, but I'm damned if I'm going to show it.
I'm ill, but I'm damned if I'm going to show it.
I'm angry, but I'm damned if I'm going to show it.
I'm in love, but I'm damned if I'm going to show it.
I'm happy, but I'm damned if I'm going to show it.
I'm scared, but I'm damned if I'm going to show it.
I'm on the run from the police, but I'm damned if I'm going
to show it.
I'm a spy, but I'm damned if I'm going to show it.

Acting the cover-up can often be more interesting and
revealing than merely demonstrating the underlying
emotion or situation. It is amazing how far you can go with
covering-up, especially if the story-line is strong enough for
the audience to know what's going on.

The Story ⌣⋅

Never stop telling yourself the story of the play, for this will illumine the story of your character within it: it will tell you what *happens* to him, and how much he is altered by the circumstances.

Each scene will have a story. An excellent television director, David Reid, used to start the early rehearsals of every scene by telling the actors the story-so-far, like TV announcers do for the later episodes of a classic serial. And he used to say: "So. That's the situation at the beginning of the scene. At the end of it the difference will be..."

The scene *travels*, therefore. It has, or should have, a starting point and a destination.

When I was rehearsing the last scene of *Professional Foul*, the scene in which John Shrapnel (Professor McKendrick) and I (Professor Anderson) were flying back from Prague to London, Tom Stoppard was very dissatisfied with the way I was doing it.

"You're too smug," he said, "too light. It's a more serious scene. You should be more concerned about Chetwyn, that he's been held by the customs officer at the airport, and isn't allowed to travel home with you."

66

"More serious?" I said.

"Yes," he said.

So I did the scene more seriously.

"Well?" I said.

"It's still not right," he said.

"Why?" I said.

"It's too serious," he said.

"But you said you ..."

"Yes, I know," he said, "but I can't write a play which starts as a comedy and ends as a tragedy."

"So you want me less serious?" I said, lost.

"No, not at the beginning of the scene."

"Ah," I said, inspired, "you mean I should travel further?"

"Yes," he said.

So I started seriously, concerned, found a moment for a change of mood, and ended flippantly.

"That's it," he said, "travel further. Good."

Telling yourself, or having the director tell you, the story-so-far is especially valuable for filming. Shooting out of sequence always bothers me, but if the story is in everyone's mind mistakes are less frequently made. And I don't mean just physical mistakes, concerning the state of clothes or the tidiness of hair or the dirtiness of hands, but emotional ones too.

The Before And After Of Each Scene ⌁

Clifford Evans, in *The Power Game*, always wanted to know what had happened immediately before a scene started. We used to invent little scenes (one of the many uses of improvisation, this) to lead up to the scene we were about to rehearse. Oh, how doing this helped us decide what to do!

And afterwards he would say: "Now, if this scene had gone on, what would have happened?" and just asking this made the end-line seem not like an end-line at all, and prevented that curious foreknowledge an audience has that a scene has finished.

The Before And After Of Each Speech ·—·

An audience can often tell not only when the end of a scene has arrived, but when the end of a speech has, too; you have signalled it somehow, and they know you have got nothing more to say and it's the other person's turn. Of course, in everyday life we often do signal to our family, friends and acquaintances that we have finished, but a lot of the time *we would have gone on talking if someone hadn't interrupted us.*

In your play, what would you have said if the other character hadn't interrupted you?

Similarly, what launches you into interrupting the other character?

Words In Brackets ⟿

I was working with Patience Collier on some of the parts she played for the Royal Shakespeare Company, and she found the addition of words in brackets to a speech could clarify its meaning and colour its intentions. (These words in brackets are not to be spoken, of course, they are merely aids to spontaneity.)

Here's a speech, not by Shakespeare but by me, just to illustrate the sort of work we did and the sort of phrases we invented. Here it is without words in brackets.

She to him: "You said that to me on my birthday last year. We were in Brighton, and we'd been for a walk through the Lanes. It was just getting dark and we'd had tea in a little café. I thought I would never forgive you, but I did, and I do now. But please don't say it again. I forgive you now, but I won't again."

There are two main ingredients of this speech: a memory and a request. A simple memory and a simple request may be all that is required, but possible, illuminating, words in brackets could be:

"(*Now I come to think of it:*) You said that to me on my birthday last year. (*Do you remember?*) We were in Brighton, and we'd been for a walk through the Lanes. (*Oh yes, I've just remembered:*) It was just getting dark and we'd had tea in a little café. (*Anyway, getting back to what I was saying:*) I thought I would never forgive you, but I did, and (*do you know?*) I do now. (*But mark my words:*) But please don't say it again. (*As I said:*) I forgive you now, but I won't again."

Spontaneity ⌁

This and the next few pieces are attempts to help you
with the most difficult but essential task for an actor: the
achievement of spontaneity. And spontaneity has to be
achieved, it has to be worked at, for the trouble with being in a
play is that you know it so well. You know the words, you
know the business, you know the story, you know the moves.
And you know everybody else's words and moves too. And
yet you have to give the illusion that you are doing it and
thinking it for the first time.

I said earlier in this book that we actors are a critical lot;
but we are always disarmed when we see a performance of
supreme spontaneity. "How does she do it?" I think, every
time I see Celia Johnson, the past-mistress of the art of
spontaneity in acting. Many of the actors in the better
television soap-operas (*Coronation Street* and *Emmerdale Farm*)
are wonderfully good at it too; but so are a lot of performers.
"You are so truthful, it's hard to believe you've ever done it
before" is a compliment we would all like receive.

A starting point can be to comb through your part for
the bits which are easy to say and the bits which are difficult.

Easy bits might be:

72

Things your character often says, from habit.

Things which are not new to him (you will have to decide what those are).

Small talk.

Things which require no switch of attention.

Things which require no change of mood.

Difficult bits might be:

Things your character has never thought of before.

Approaches to other characters involving hesitancy.

Ideas your character is trying to clarify.

You will find lots of examples in every worthwhile part, and it is worthwhile making the effort to discover them.

Preambles ⟶

The performances which sound least spontaneous are those in which every sentence sounds like a statement of intent. Nothing gets thrown away, nothing is rushed over, nothing is slack; and the performance therefore seems wooden and heavy. One way of preventing this is to underline in your script the really important statements you make, or questions you ask, and to use what you can of the preceding dialogue as a preamble.

In the following speech every sentence could be given equal weight, in which case the final question, the pivot of the speech and the reason for its existence, would go for nothing.

"It's cold today. That's why I'm so well wrapped up. But it's warm in here. Do you mind if I take my coat off? It's always so snug here. It feels comfortable. Always. How lucky you are to live here. How's Harry?"

Treat the earlier part as a preamble, distracted, knowing that eventually you have got to ask how Harry is, and it's different kettle of fish.

Forget ∽

Flora Robson, in *Black Chiffon* at the Westminster Theatre and *The House By the Lake* at the Duke of York's Theatre, was the first actress I ever saw who electrified the audience by appearing not to know what she was going to say next. She was apparently so distraught that her mind went blank; only gradually did she recover.

It's a risky business, drying deliberately; but it's worth it occasionally.

Feel For Words ✎

Certainly I think it's good to hunt around in your mind for the right word, from time to time. We often have to search for words in everyday life, so why not do the same in plays?

Ers and ums can be added too, providing they are properly motivated and not merely a mannerism. And I like it when an actor back-tracks in a speech to add a word he has omitted. Say the written sentence is: "I feel very distressed about what you've just told me." A good "actor's addition" could be: "I feel dist—very distressed about what you've just told me." "Very" becomes a more important word thereby. All this, of course, applies to modern, realistic plays. It would be a bit dangerous in Shakespeare!

New Move On A New Thought ⌐⌐

This has already been a title in this book, but I feel I must use it again here, for it is a splendid aid to spontaneity. A new thought, as I said, comes with energy, and that energy can be channelled into a move. The move can be big or small; it can be just a sudden look.

As a simple example, imagine a man talking to two others who are standing on either side of him. He starts a sentence by looking at one of them, and during the sentence his gaze drifts off into the space between them. At the beginning of the next sentence he suddenly looks at the other hearer, and drifts off, mid-sentence, again. At the beginning of the third sentence he looks at his first hearer again. And so on. It is too mechanical, of course, to go from one to the other alternately like that—one hearer is usually more important than the other. But it will suffice for this imaginary exercise.

To convert it into a real one, try this speech of Casca's in *Julius Caesar*. It was very well done by the actor in the BBC Television Shakespeare series: Sam Dastor was talking to Richard Pasco as Brutus and David Collings as Cassius. Brutus says:

77

"Tell us the manner of it, gentle Casca."

Casca replies:

"I can as well be hang'd as tell the manner of it: it was mere foolery; I did not mark it. I saw Mark Antony offer him a crown—yet 'twas not a crown neither, 'twas one of those coronets—and, as I told you, he put it by once; but for all that, to my thinking, he would fain have had it. Then he offered it to him again; then he put it by again; but to my thinking he was very loath to lay his fingers off it. And then he offered it the third time; he put it the third time by; and still as he refus'd it, the rabblement hooted, and clapp'd their chopt hands, and threw up their sweaty night-caps, and uttered such a deal of stinking breath because Caesar refus'd the crown, that it had almost choked Caesar; for he swooned and fell down at it. And for mine own part I durst not laugh, for fear of opening my lips and receiving the bad air."

Interrupted Actions ⟶

You are about to drink but you don't drink because
something has occurred to you. You are about to smoke but
you don't smoke because you've suddenly thought of
something you want to say. You are about to sit but you
don't sit because you've seen something out of place on the
mantelpiece.

Interrupted actions: a wonderful aid to spontaneity. I
learned about them from watching Humphrey Bogart. Over
and over again, in his films, the glass of whisky would be
raised to his lips, but he didn't drink, not just yet, not until
he'd made one more laconic remark. Then he'd drink.

Look, Move, Speak ⌣·

Actions happen in the order: look, move, speak; or, more deeply: idea, confirmation of idea, utterance of idea.

If you feel unspontaneous in a part, the application of this formula may provide the remedy.

A nice homework exercise for this is to pretend that you are showing a prospective buyer round your home, pointing out its features, good and bad, and its contents (you're selling the lot, lock, stock and barrel!). Be quite conscious of looking at a thing, pointing and/or moving to it, and talking about it, in that order.

Then, as a further exercise, show some people round an imaginary place: you could be talking about a beautiful view from the top of a hill, say, or showing them round a garden. See the objects, indicate them with a move, and speak about them.

"Look, move, speak," I used to say at RADA, "and you can't go wrong."

Well, you can. But every little helps.

Get Your First Scene Set •~•

As soon as you can, get your first scene set. It's often quite a task, this, because your first scene is rarely the easiest (in fact I often find it the hardest of the lot), but your mood at later rehearsals, and during the recording, if it's television, or the performance, if it's theatre, will be determined by how well you think you have done it. It's worth making quite sure it's as secure as iron.

Later scenes you can leave a little more to chance. But do not risk it with the first one.

Act Sideways ⌁

Have you ever thought that the essential difference between acting in the theatre and acting in front of cameras is that in the theatre you need to *widen* your performance so the whole audience can see you, whereas for the cameras you need to narrow it down?

In the theatre, the actor is the apex of a triangle and the audience is the base-line:

ACTOR

AUDIENCE

In television and films, the actor is the base-line, and the audience is the apex:

ACTOR

AUDIENCE

Acting sideways, then, is for the theatre. It is necessary for you to open out your performance, to use "anchors", to "talk off" people, and to use the fourth wall properly.

The Fourth Wall •—•

If the set-designer had designed the fourth wall, what would he have put there? What is there to look at? You will have to agree with the other actors about this, but it's worth discussing.

Technically the fourth wall is there to receive the thoughts for which you do not need to look directly at the other players. And technically the easiest level for your eyes is the darkest part of the auditorium, just below the Dress Circle; in most theatres that will be your own eye-level.

Play The Opposite ⌐

A: How are you today?

B: Oh, marvellous, thank you. Yes, I feel really good today.

A (turning to C): And how are you?

C: Oh, dreadful. I've got a terrible headache. I couldn't sleep last night. No, I feel dreadful.

B *could* be solemn-faced, quite serious. Because he is *saying* how he feels, he has no need to demonstrate it.

Likewise C could smile, or even laugh. Because he's saying how he feels, he has no need to demonstrate it.

Play the opposite! Notice how often you do this in everyday life ...

A: What do you think of it so far?

B (solemnly, frowning): Wonderful!

A: And you?

C (laughing): Terrible!

Be Monotonous ~

"For God's sake be monotonous!" said Alan Bridges, when he was rehearsing Greer Garson and me in a scene from *Crown Matrimonial* (we were doing the television version). "You actors, you're all the same: you're all so good at *explaining* the text ... you've got the right inflections, the right emphases, you know exactly what you mean and you're determined to let us know. Come on, you two,"—I looked across at Greer to see how she was taking all this, and was relieved to see that she was still smiling— "come on, you two, for God's sake Stop Acting! Mumble! Mutter! Anything ... but don't explain it all!"

So we did. And it was wonderful.

I never do a play without remembering his golden advice. Mind you: care, care, care! It's a corrective to be used against being over-emphatic. If your speech is already monotonous, quickly turn the page!

Telephone Conversations ⌒

If it's a two-way conversation (as it often is in television plays or films) it is easy enough. The hard thing is when you are on your own.

It certainly is worthwhile (of course it is) to invent and write down what the other person says; and I think the main trick about doing telephone conversations is to give the other person time to say what he has to say, but only just. If you don't give him enough time, well, the conversation will have no truth in it and the audience will dismiss you; if you give him too much time, you will be boring and the audience will get restless.

It's a curious thing, being just one end of a telephone conversation: you have to bring the other person to life for the audience; you are doing the acting for two, as it were, for the price of one. So let the other person interrupt you, if you can; and interrupt him; and talk at the same time. This makes him very vivid.

If you interrupt him, you have to stop him talking, so go a little louder. If he interrupts you, let him do so on a consonant. It is much easier to stop at a consonant than it is on a vowel. If your sentence is

"I'm not sure I could manage that," and he interrupts you, it is easier to say

"I'm not sure I could m ..." than

"I'm not sure I could ma ..."

I don't know why, but I think it's because "I'm not sure I could ma ..." will result in a glottal stop, and will not sound (or feel) nearly as convincing.

Try laughing, if it is apt, at something the unseen person says. It's quite hard to do, this, and needs practice. I have no tips at all for laughing, but it is, of course, something you must be able to do; but oh, when you bring it off, how it convinces the audience there is somebody there at the other end of the line!

Dialling is always a problem because it takes so long. Again, you cannot cheat—if it's a London number, and you're in London, you must dial seven digits, and if it's a long distance call you must dial even more, and you must start with 0! What you *can* do, though, to speed up the whole dreary business, is choose the lower numbers for as many of the digits as possible. So a Birmingham number could be, 021-422-1311.

And, usually, hold the mouthpiece low enough for the audience to see your mouth. It looks better.

Do Not Cheat ⌐

There are many other activities which, like listening on the telephone, should not be cheated.

Writing, for example. Those hurried squiggles we have all seen, usually in period plays, really will not do. A period character sits at a period desk with period parchment and a period quill pen, and he says aloud what he is writing and says it so quickly in an effort not to be boring that you *know* he can't possibly be writing the actual words he is speaking. And sometimes he writes without even bothering to form letters and you *know* that what's on the parchment is:

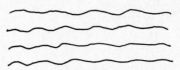

Reading must not be cheated either. If you've got to read a letter silently, well, you've got to read it. Quickly; but you've got to do it. If you have to look at a list of figures and come to a conclusion about, say, a customer's account, you have got to look at it and have time for the assessment. I remember the producer of *Telford's Change*, Mark Shivas, saying to me at a rehearsal: "I don't believe you could have read all those figures in Maddox's account. I mean, in the story you've never seen them before, have you? They are news to you."

"But Mark," I said, "it'll take so long."

"Never mind," he said, "you've got to do it!"

If you are going to gossip about somebody who is leaving the room, you must wait until they have gone out and closed the door, or are out of earshot, before you start. "Oh, I can't wait that long," you may complain.

"But you must," the director should say.

Exits And Entrances ⌁

When you exit you are going somewhere else.

When you enter you have come from somewhere else. Where?

Someone once told me, I think it was Nigel Patrick, that it can be a good idea sometimes to be in the middle of doing something as you enter, like putting a handkerchief back in your pocket; it means no more than that you have blown your nose in the place from which you have come, but at least it means you did *something* there. If you're coming from upstairs, I suppose you could just be finishing putting on your jacket or cardigan or whatever. It makes "upstairs" a bit more vivid.

But it is to be used sparingly, this.

Drinking ∼

A lot of drinking goes on in plays. If it's a nice middle-class room, there's bound to be a drinks table somewhere. The director will want one anyway because it will help him with the moves. But have you noticed how, with all that drinking going on, the actors seem to remain stone-cold sober? Actors are either sober or drunk (in "Drunk scenes"). There are lots of states in between which are worth exploring.

Incidentally, if you breathe in before you drink you cannot choke.

Eating ～

Quite a lot of eating goes on in plays, too. Especially in television plays. And commercials. How do the actors do it, I often wonder, when they have to do retake after retake of eating a chocolate bar? In plays, well, you have got to eat; but the trick is to eat the easiest foods—the mashed potato, for example, rather than the meat, which can be so very, very chewy and embarrassing—and to have smaller quantities on your fork or in your spoon than you would in everyday life. For some unfathomable reason it takes longer to eat in plays than it does in everyday life, and it is harder to swallow. "Will it never go down?" one so often thinks to oneself.

Smoking ⁓

A lot of smoking goes on, too, though it is nice to note that writers and directors are now far more loath to insist that you smoke if you are a non-smoker, because they know that you can't smoke in plays unless you smoke in everyday life: it will look all wrong and it will make you dizzy. Of course, if you are in *Who's Afraid of Virginia Woolf?* you will just have to smoke, and there are herbal cigarettes on the market now which make it more bearable for a non-smoker.

An odd thing about smoking in plays is that it's harder to *taste* the smoke. So to confirm that your cigarette is alight, puff out the first intake of smoke straight away. You (and the audience) can then *see* that it is alight, and you (and the audience) can relax.

James Mason said to me, when we were doing a scene in a film called *Tiara Tahiti*, "Never smoke in films." This was after he had witnessed my appalling discomfort in the scene. For each take of each angle, I had to light up again; my mouth was so dry at the end of the day I could hardly speak and wanted to vomit. Continuity problems are acute, too. "Sorry, sorry, sorry," I would have to say, stopping a take for an agonising moment: "my cigarette's not the right length.

I'd smoked about half of it by now, hadn't I?" So a cigarette would be broken in two, and the frayed end would flare up in flames as I lit it.

James Mason was right. "I never do," he said.

Switching Things On And Off ⌣

Usually lights, lamps, radio sets and other gadgets are operated by someone else. The lighting people will be doing the lights, the sound people will be doing the radio sets.

Well, if they switch things on or off *before* you have actually got there, there's nothing you can do except look a Charlie. You'll look a Charlie, too, if there is a long delay after your hand has gone to the switch. But here you can save yourself by not giving all your attention to the switch. You can go up to the switch and, having touched it, look away from it (talking or listening the while, or just looking at something else); that half-mind left on the switch accounts for the delay.

Bad Dialogue ⌒

A few tips now about how to deal with poor dialogue. It is not only in films or television where an actor has to face this problem, but these are the two media where it is most prevalent.

Most importantly, I think, I would advise that if you can bring yourself to say the lines, do, rather than try to alter them. Time and again I have seen a scene get worse instead of better as actors nit-pick over the words. And it's terribly time-consuming, too. My least favourite rehearsals are those which develop into script conferences between the director and the actors.

Of course, sometimes you have got to change the lines, particularly in a television series where a new author has been brought in and gets facts wrong about the story and about the characters and their idiosyncrasies.

But a lot of dialogue is much more speakable than many actors allow. A bad line can be made to sound almost like a good one, provided an actor has a very clear attitude towards it: an attitude which prevents it from being a mere statement of fact. How often a line can be saved by the attitude:

(This is not really how I want to put this, but ...)
We're back to "words in brackets", and other helpful ones
are:

        (I know it's a cliché but ...)
        (You'll probably think this is funny but ...)
        (I'm talking nonsense, I know, but ...)
        (Look, I'm trying not to be intense; let me put it to
you lightly and quickly:)

Actors' Additions ~

True and original attitudes towards the words you speak and the people you are addressing are fundamental to dealing with poor dialogue, but even after days of struggling you may feel inadequate and defeated. What to do? Well, a number of things you might be able to add could just yield the silk purse you are looking for.

Drunkenness, for example. Could you be drunk in this scene you are faced with? Among other things, drunkenness allows you to switch more violently from one emotion to another, releases your anger and your tears, excuses you' from making coherent sense, and it is interesting in itself! I was once driven to using drunkenness to get away with appalling dialogue (I dare not mention here in which play!) and it seemed to work: the rubbish I had to say was apparently caused by drink. Drink talks, as they say.

Tiredness is another useful addition (rarely used). Tiredness, or illness even, can mean that only half your mind is on what you are saying and hearing: there will be an abstracted air about you; and, like drunkenness, tiredness is interesting in itself.

Jollity, too, can cover many a cliché, and has one

99

advantage over drunkenness and tiredness: it will make you act quickly. Speed can be a life-saver in awkward passages.

Laughter can sometimes help. I often think we laugh more in everyday life than we do in plays; why not even it up a bit?

Temperature is a nice addition, too. How hot are you? How cold? When the door opens is there a draught? Being cold can yield more for you than the clichéd rubbing of hands and warming them at the fire, and being hot more than the clichéd mopping of the brow and neck with a handkerchief.

You don't need to wait for poor dialogue, of course, to employ some of these additions. They are good for good stuff as well.

Secondary Tasks ⟶•

"I'm going to make it hard for you," said Alan Bridges, when we were rehearsing *Crown Matrimonial*. "You actors, you always have it so easy in plays. I'm going to make it hard. Now, let's see. You're talking to Queen Mary and the Princess Royal and there's a fire in the grate. You know that bit where you're just about to say you love Mrs Simpson, well, what if a piece of coal fell out of the fire and rolled dangerously near to the carpet?"

"Oh no, Alan, not *then*! It's my best bit."

"Yes, why not? Could happen. I mean, if a piece of coal rolls away from a fire someone's got to get the tongs and put it back. Haven't they? Otherwise the carpet will catch fire."

"Oh, Alan ..."

"Try it!"

I did, and, at the second attempt, we all agreed it was really rather good. It didn't interrupt the scene, it took the expectedness out of the moment, and converted it into one of surprise.

I like secondary tasks. Well chosen, they can give surprising new colours to a scene:

Two people are talking, but reading at the same time.

Two people are talking, but washing up at the same time, or laying the table, or dressing, or undressing, or cooking, or eating, or looking at a view, or walking along, or being overheard, or having a rest, or doing exercises, or dancing, or dusting, or playing games, or working at something.

Overlaps ⌁

Alan Bridges also likes overlaps. "If you can answer before Queen Mary finished her speech, do; talk while she's still talking."

"Do you mind, Greer?" I said, "because I don't want it to throw you."

"No, of course not," she said, "I think it's good."

"There you are, you see," said Alan, triumphant, "you've both just done it. Greer answered, "No, of course not" to your question, "Do you mind, Greer?" The fact that you went on speaking did not stop Greer from interrupting you, nor did it stop you from finishing what you wanted to say. You've just done it. So do it in the play."

Used sparingly, I like overlaps too.

Criticism ᴗ

Everyone has faults, and it is good to have them pointed out occasionally by the director or by friends. If the fault is one which applies to your acting in general, as opposed to just your performance in the play, do take special heed and work as hard as you can to eradicate it.

People may tell you that you fade out at the ends of sentences, that your speech is not clear enough, that you blink too much, that you fidget, that you smile too much, that you don't smile enough, that you don't listen properly, that you gesture too much, that you don't gesture enough, that you're content with too little, that you complicate things unnecessarily, that your hair-style doesn't suit you, that you've got a funny walk.

Listen, and work!

But don't listen to everybody. Rely on the director and close friends. If you listen to everybody you will get awfully confused, for you will hear so many different things. If you are very, very good everybody will say so and have similar reasons for thinking so. If you are very, very bad everybody will say so, behind your back, and have similar reasons for thinking so. But if you are somewhere in between very, very good and very, very bad, which is where most of us are most of the time, everybody will know that all is not perfect, but will have differing reasons for thinking so.

It's as well to remember, always, that you can't please everybody.

Bad Rehearsals ∾

There will always be those days when, in spite of all the work you have put in, in spite of all the ideas you have thrown into the melting pot with the director and the company, nothing seems to come of it: self-consciousness takes over, concentration becomes impossible, your face freezes, your arms and legs are as heavy as lead, and you feel that your very talent is in danger of disappearing, as you would like to, through the rehearsal room floor. I have seen actors and actresses of great distinction weep from the sheer panic and embarrassment caused by such feelings. And you never really know what sets them off; it can be anything: you might be tired, off-colour, worried about something at home; or it may be that somebody new has come into the rehearsal room and is watching you before you feel ready to be watched. It can, as I said, be anything.

These days are dangerous, and hard to recover from. But they do have one advantage: they make you go home and WORK.

Further Homework ⌁

The Mirror ⸺

Should you use it?

It is good for correcting pointed-out faults, for the sight of them in the mirror will confirm that they exist.

Certainly I do not agree with those who say you should never use it. It provides a very useful check, particularly on bits you have found awkward. "Oh, of course," you say to your reflection, "I'm standing in the wrong way for this bit: I should face you squarely, feet and all, shoulders and all, not just turn my head sideways to you and look at you over my shoulder." Pictures of yourself looking wrong will help you to start looking right. And then you will start feeling right.

Fluffing ⌒

If, in rehearsal, you have fluffed a line several times, or if you fear you might fluff it, or if it's just hard to say, it's worth taking it out of context and practising it over and over again like a tongue-twister.

The most noticeable mistake an actor can make is a fluff. An audience might not know you have dried, they *might* not know you have giggled, but they will always know you have fluffed.

And while I'm on the subject of tongue-twisters, I think it's worth being able to do a few really well; you can always use them as warm-ups before a performance. All RADA students who were taught by the late Clifford Turner will remember what emphasis he put on "quick diction exercises", and will be able to do his favourite:

> Lah-lay-lee-lay-lah-law-loo-law
> Lah-lay-lee-lay-lah-law-loo-law

and on and on, over and over, at breakneck speed. It gets the tongue moving, just as "Peter Piper" gets the lips.

Reality Tests—1 ᕫ

With the constant pressure of rehearsals, when you have to go over and over each scene, thinking of so many details, making alterations, cuts and additions, coming to conclusions, it is very easy to lose your instinct. You had it when you first started, but now you've lost it, and cannot see the wood for the trees. You've got to get it back.

Doing "reality tests" at home is one way. It's curious how well they work and, thankfully, they are quite amusing to do, too.

Go through the words of your part, aloud, but change the circumstances. For example, whatever the scene, do it this time with a duster in your hand, and clean the room. Place the other character or characters in chairs, so you know where they are, and do the scene while you are dusting.

It will tell you many things, this exercise: it will tell you when your concentration can be mostly on the dusting and you needn't look at the other characters; it will also tell you when you *have* to look at them and stop dusting. So, for the play, it will tell you when you must look at the other characters when you needn't. It will freshen up the dialogue too.

You will think of many variations on this exercise: a good one is to be working in one room—washing up, or making a bed, or just sitting reading—and saying all your lines to someone who is in another one; you are talking through the walls, as it were, to someone you cannot see. If your instinct is really returning to you, you may find that at some moment you have to leave what you are doing and go into the other room to say something to them directly. But leave them as soon as you can, for your secondary task is very important, and you want to get back to it.

Reality Tests—2 ·~·

The idea behind these reality tests is to keep some things the same but alter others in order to bring back your instinct.

This time, try changing the people you are talking to. Try saying the whole part as though to your oldest friend.

No, try it! You'll be surprised!

Reality Tests—3 ·~·

This is John Hurt's idea, and it is very good. Instead of acting your part, tell the story of the scenes, including your lines and what you can remember of the other characters', to an imaginary person (or a real one, if you want) sitting in a chair. Your story will sound something like this:

"So he comes up to me and says, where were you last night at eighty thirty, and I say to him, oh, well, I was having dinner out with some friends, and he looks very suspicious and says, would I mind telling him their names, and for a moment I want to refuse but I realise that if I do it will make me look guilty, and of course I'm not, so I tell him their names, and the name of the restaurant ..." and so on.

This exercise will tell you where you have been overacting, and remind you of the true content of each scene.

Reality Tests—4 ⟿

If a line or speech just won't come right, change the words. Put it in your own words. Improvise.

It would be very tedious to do this for your whole part, but for those sticky bits you may find, when you go back to the author's words, they feel a bit fresher.

Never Bring A Sick Mind To A Part ⁓

Richard Gatehouse, who was with me at Sheffield rep. in the early fifties, said: "If you're not feeling well, or just not in the mood, don't work. It could do more harm than good. Never bring a sick mind to a part."

And often it's amazing what a good rest and an early night will do!

Final Rehearsals ⌇

Pace ∙∽∙

This will be the word on everyone's lips now. The play will probably need to be speeded up.

Lionel Harris used to say, at one of the final run-throughs, "Everybody, when we go through the play this time, I would like you to go too fast … I don't mean gabble, but just a little too fast for comfort." And when the run-through was over he would invariably say: "Good. That was about the right speed for the play."

A play should always be acted as quickly as possible, though "as possible" is very much the controller of that dictum. Some bits are bound to be slow; but cues can often be more sharply taken, changes of tone more surprisingly used, and the four varieties of speech more vividly brought into play.

The Four Varieties ⌁

Speed, pitch, volume and tone.

And the one most frequently under-used is "speed".

It is all too easy to get a uniform speed for a part—fast, leisurely, slow—and stick to it. And although in everyday life people are slow- or fast-speakers, nevertheless, within that generality, the speed at which we speak is changing all the time; and whenever this variety can be used in a play, it should be. Along with the other three, of course.

They do help to stop an audience being bored.

And they help an overall sense of pace, because coming-in-on-cue, which everyone knows is desirable, is quite all right if you don't take the other person's speed, pitch, volume or tone.

Don't Pause ᵔ

"Don't pause!" said Edith Evans when she was giving a lecture to RADA students in the Vanbrugh Theatre, and she looked sternly about. "Never pause!" And she paused, giving our disbelief ample time to register. "Young actors nowadays are always pausing," she said, "and I don't like it. You see, if you pause you are saying to the audience: Ladies and Gentlemen, this pause is more interesting than the author's next line. Now, if you *can* say that and *mean* it, *then* you can pause."

A change of tone is a good substitute for a pause. Suppose the dialogue to be:

A: Did you enjoy today's rehearsal?

B: Yes. No.

Between "Yes" and "No" there is, for whatever reason, a complete change of heart. It could be easy enough to have a really long think between the words. And in certain circumstances that may be what is required. But if the two words sound completely different, if, for example, "Yes" is firm and loud and "No" is doubting and quiet, you will be able to cut the pause to a minimum.

Just one more thought about pausing. Never forget that

121

if you pause, either before or during a speech, everyone else is pausing with you. They cannot speak because the author has not given them anything to say. How often one has heard an actor plead with another:

"Look, boy, if you pause there, I'd come in, I'd say something ... I mean, I've got egg on my face during that pause ... do you need it?"

The answer has to be "No".

Give The Scene To The Other Actor ⟿

This is another of John Hurt's ideas, and it's very relaxing. Concentrate on the other people rather than on yourself. After all, this is what you do in everyday life; you might as well do it in plays.

"Chuck it to them," he said, "and say to yourself: it's their scene, not mine.

"But if it really *is* your scene, grab it!"

Comedy —

This is the subject I dreaded teaching at RADA. A joke is only really funny the first time, and after five people have tried it there's no laughter left. The classes in comedy were the glummest of the lot.

And it's such an idiosyncratic subject, too, so much to do with personality and flair, that it's very hard to talk about. Athene Seyler's book *The Craft of Comedy* is as good as you'll get.

I can only say, "Watch comedians! Learn from those who appeal to you!" I learned a lot from acting with Penelope Keith in *Donkeys' Years*. She is a fine comedienne and a remarkably truthful actress. She never strains for comic effect. Truth comes first.

But there are one or two things all good comedians do which are perhaps worth listing here:

Speak clearly and brightly.

Don't fade out at the ends of sentences.

Keep the rhythm of the lines. Keep the flow of the feed-lines and the laugh-lines right through to the very last word. Remember that when you have a laugh-line you are not only inviting the audience to laugh but you are inviting them to

124

laugh at a particular moment ... that moment, usually the last word of your line, could do with an extra little punch.

Don't be slow.

Don't try to be funny but know what it is that's funny about the funny bits.

Be as relaxed as possible, and know the value of slack turns of the head during a laugh-line. I don't know why they work but they seem to, as do small involuntary movements like crossing your legs, rubbing your eyes, putting your hand to your forehead, wiping ash off your jacket, putting a glass down, taking a drink, taking a puff of a cigar—remember George Burns and Groucho Marx?—taking your glasses off, putting them on, anything except stroking the lobe of your ear: that's the only one which has become such a cliché it's unforgivable.

Sense the house: laughter is largely a matter of audience-temperature, hence the phrase "warming them up". Use as much energy as the part can stand.

"Timing" is a difficult thing to write about: it is so much a matter of sensing. What most people mean by "timing" is using a beat-pause between the feed-line and the laugh-line, but of course it depends very much on the meaning of the lines; it can often be just as funny to come in on cue.

But let me give an example.

One of my favourite comedy sequences was near the beginning of *Donkeys' Years*, when Christopher Headingley (a politician) and David Buckle (a doctor) meet, after twenty years, at a reunion party at their old university. They don't know what to say to each other. Here is the dialogue, as written by Michael Frayn:

HEADINGLEY: Well. How *are* you, and so on?

BUCKLE: Well, all right, Christopher. Not too bad. In quite good working order. And you?

HEADINGLEY: Oh, fine. Fine, fine, fine, fine, fine, fine.

BUCKLE: Oh, good.

HEADINGLEY:	Yes, fine.
BUCKLE:	Oh, good. Good, good, good, good, good, good.
HEADINGLEY:	Fine.
BUCKLE:	Good.
HEADINGLEY:	And you're ... sawing people up?
BUCKLE:	That's right! Whhht! Out with their waterworks!
HEADINGLEY:	My word.
BUCKLE:	And you're ... Parliamentary Under-Secretary, is that what they call it, at the Ministry of, isn't it in fact Education?
HEADINGLEY:	Whhht! Off with their heads.
BUCKLE:	Goodness me.
HEADINGLEY:	Tell the Vice-Chancellor where he gets off.
BUCKLE:	Well, well, well.

pause

Here it is again, with notes on the timing which Peter Jeffrey and I eventually found secured the most laughs.

HEADINGLEY:	Well. How *are* you, and so on?
BUCKLE:	(*brightly*) Well, all right, Christopher. (*tick pause*) Not too bad. (*pause, then equally brightly*) In quite good working order. (*longer pause, lost*) And you?
HEADINGLEY:	(*immediately*) Oh fine. (*pause, lost; while thinking of something to say, absently:* Fine, fine, fine, fine, fine, fine.
BUCKLE:	(*immediately*) Oh, good.
HEADINGLEY:	(*pause, louder, reassuringly*) Yes, fine.
BUCKLE:	(*immediately, reassured*) Oh, good. (*pause, lost; while thinking of something to say, absently:*) Good, good, good, good, good, good.

HEADINGLEY:	(*slight pause, while getting the next question sorted out*) Fine.
BUCKLE:	(*immediately*) Good.
HEADINGLEY:	(*more or less immediately, depending on the audience's laughter*) And you're ... sawing people up?
BUCKLE:	(*immediately*) That's right! Whhht! Out with their waterworks!
HEADINGLEY:	(*immediately, impressed*) My word.
BUCKLE:	(*pause; slowly, not at all sure he's right*) And you're ... Parliamentary Under-Secretary, is that what they call it, at the Ministry of, isn't it in fact Education?
HEADINGLEY:	(*immediately, wittily*) Whhht! Off with their heads!
BUCKLE:	(*immediately, impressed*) Goodness me.
HEADINGLEY:	(*laughing, loudly*) Tell the Vice-Chancellor where he gets off.
BUCKLE:	(*laughing*) Well, well, well.
	Pause. Both lost.

Walking away after a laugh-line (the laugh-line's "aftersurge"!) can help: Morecambe and Wise often do this; and I suppose ideally a feed-line should be slightly louder than a laugh-line, but the reverse can often work, and really, it's impossible to lay down laws, but what I *do* know is that it is necessary to be good at comedy in your own way because all the skills you develop from it will be useful for your acting in general, and when you come to think of it all our very best actors are very good at comedy.

Having got a laugh, incidentally, remember that while the audience is laughing you are pausing—the laughter does not *belong* to the stage—and the pause must be filled.

And come in with the next line as the laughter is dying. Do not wait for it to finish.

Relax ◦—•

Now you are getting near to the performance, and are concentrating on polish and pace and comedy and attack and team-work, you should balance all this with a conscious attempt to be as relaxed as possible, especially in those bits you have struggled over. A tension may have crept in and you may be able to do with a gesture or two fewer, a delivery less emphatic. Your first scene in particular may well benefit from a dose of relaxation. I always like it when an audience is led gently into the world of the play, and if a first scene is too "acted", too loud, unnecessarily quick, the audience will be put off, and it will take them a long time to recover.

Do A Rehearsal For Something ⌁

Lionel Harris again.

"Now everybody," he would say, clapping his hands for attention—he always called the cast "everybody"—"I want you to do this run-through for listening. Don't think of anything else except listening. Remember: by now you already know what everybody else says to you. It's so easy to anticipate your reply. Really listen, right up to their last syllable.

"Everybody: this time I want you to pretend you've never said any of it before. Do this rehearsal for spontaneity.

"Everybody: do this rehearsal for a sense of place. Where are you? What are you looking at? What is the room like? Do you know it well, or is it new to you? When you go up and down those stairs, are they stairs you know well so you don't have to look at the treads, or are they stairs you don't know at all so you have to look at the treads?"

And speed, of course. We'd do a run-through for speed.

I always derived great pleasure and amusement from his later rehearsals, although he could sometimes send one up most horribly.

"Lionel," I said, after many run-throughs of a television

play we were about to take into the studio, "Lionel, I feel I'm getting stale. Give me something new to think."

"Oh, I can't think of anything," he said, crossly, "make up something for yourself." A moment's pause, while he made sure the cast was listening. "No, *I* know," he said softly, a smile just beginning to show on his face, "do it," and he paused again, looking furtively round at everyone else, "do it as though you are wearing an enormous picture-hat."

I don't think we got through that rehearsal.

Emotion ↜

There will be other rehearsals, run-throughs, when the play seems to take off. Suddenly new things happen. Suddenly there is a flow, a continuity. Your instinct is taking over, and, with it, your emotion.

It is like making a cake: you got together all the ingredients and mixed them and refined them according to the recipe. Now all you have to do is put the mixture into the oven and let it bake. The work is done and the heat takes over. If the work has been right the cake will rise.

As Stanislavsky said: "When the inner conditions are prepared, and right, feelings will come to the surface of their own accord." Emotions have nothing to do with will. You do not will yourself to laugh, to cry, to be angry, to be ecstatic... these things happen in spite of yourself: you laugh because you cannot help it, you cry because you cannot help it, you are angry, you are ecstatic, because you cannot help it.

Let these emotions have free rein now. They will bind your performance, give it a shape. For soon it will be performance-time, and it is nice to go into the studio for the recording, or into the theatre for the First Night, knowing

131

that the cake is still rising, still in the ascendant, and the heat is doing its work.

Your memory will be at work too, allowing you to recollect the changes which are now taking place; and your taste will also hopefully be at work, telling you when your emotions are getting out of hand, and when it would be more moving to control them. Nothing is more affecting than bravery; you can will yourself to *stop* laughing, to *stop* crying, and this attempt to control yourself, this conflict between the natural expression of an emotion and a desire to control it can become the most moving part of your performance.

"All right, I'm ready now," you will say, with that mixture of longing and dread which we all have, "I'm ready for the First Night, or the television or film or radio studio, or the recording booth, or wherever. I'm ready."

And the cake comes out of the oven.

The Performance .—.

Relax And Enjoy It ∽

Your performance is determined by what you have rehearsed. If you have rehearsed well your performance will take care of itself. Just do what you have practised.

If you feel your performance take wing, let it fly—it can be the most exhilarating feeling in all the world. If it doesn't, if it remains stubbornly earth-bound, don't worry. If it's accurate it will be all right.

Try not to judge yourself: you will so often be wrong. When I watch myself on television I am always surprised. The bits I thought I did well at the recording are often my least favourite when I see them, and the bits I thought were terrible are not so bad after all.

If you judge yourself while you are performing, you are judging your present form, not the validity of the decisions you have taken during rehearsals, and it is those decisions which more than anything determine the quality of your performance.

So. Just do it. Relax and enjoy it. The *Telegraph Sunday Magazine* (25 February 1979) quotes Dorothy Tutin as saying: "Michael Bryant ... told me he looks on acting as a hobby. I thought: yes, I'll do that too. It makes such a difference.

135

Now, instead of thinking, right, I've done all the chores, now I've got to go to work, I think, good, now I can go and do my hobby."

Retakes ─•

In the film or television studio, when several takes of a scene may be recorded, it's very hard not to start comparing one with another.

I remember when Stephen Rea and I had done several takes of a long scene in a hotel corridor in *Professional Foul* he said to me, reverting from his Czech accent to his native Northern Irish one, "Oh, it's terrible, it's terrible! You do a scene once, and you just do it. You do a scene twice, and you just do it. But after that! You start judging yourself! I just couldn't do it that last time."

He could, and was brilliant; so even judging yourself is not too harmful. But what can help, in the pause between one take and another, instead of merely regretting you've got to do it again, is to think of just one bit you could do better. Aim for that. And you'll be glad to do the retake.

Rehearse/Record ⌒

    With the advent of discontinuous recording and shooting a play out of sequence, acting for television has become a very different thing. The "performance" days can be very long, sometimes over twelve hours, and I often think on those days: you know, even an uncut version of *Hamlet* is only four-and-a-half hours!

    What to do, just to keep going and keep at performance pitch?

    Three things:

    Don't waste your energy on anything but the play. It's amazing how tiring an hour's clatter-chatter in the canteen can be at meal-breaks. If you've got a lot to do, have food in your dressing-room and rest your body and your voice.

    If it's a rehearsal, don't try to do it well. It's better to do it badly. If you do it well you'll think, damn, I'll never be as good when we record it, and you'll probably be right. Just "mark it", as Ralph Richardson used to say: just go through the motions.

    If it's a recording, try and think not so much about what you are going to do but about what you have just done. Where have you come from? What did you see there? Was it

138

a view over the Yorkshire moors, or a street in Islington? If you were walking—over the moors or in the street—has that left you slightly out of breath? (It's a nice last addition, this.) And if what you are about to record is the continuation of a scene you have already embarked on, go through the last few speeches you had before this bit. You will know where you are then.

Television Cameras ～

Should you know when the camera is on you and when it's not?

Up to a point you can't help but know because when the camera is on you its little red light will go on, and when it is not it will go out, and you will see it out of the corner of your eye.

But I prefer not to notice it, if I can, and to trust the director to have noticed my moments of change in the rehearsal room and to include them in his camera-script. Well, if he doesn't, he doesn't. He obviously thought that what somebody else was doing was more interesting, or more relevant to the story, and chose that.

I used to like to know what every camera cut was, but this can lead, as Gordon Jackson puts it, to "clunk-click" acting: every time the camera cuts to you you feel you must do something, so you nod, or open your eyes a little wider, or do some sort of reaction. "Cut!" says the director. "React!" says your mind.

No. On the whole I prefer to forget the cameras as much as possible, and to get back to what Lionel Harris told me so many years ago: "Don't try to convince the camera: try to convince the people you are with."

140

Filming ⌁

Although television is becoming more and more like filming there is one big difference, and that it that for a television play you will have spent days or weeks rehearsing for it, whereas for filming you will be lucky if you have rehearsed in advance at all.

So the main thing, I think, is to know the lines backwards, forwards and inside out, so that the small amount of time you spend rehearsing before you shoot will not throw you into consternation. You will be able to give all your attention to the circumstances of the scene and the contributions of the other people; and you will more easily find time for working out the details of your movements, so that continuity is not just the prerogative of the Continuity Girl. "Was this parcel in my left hand or right hand?" She will be able to answer you, but it's quite nice not to have to ask.

The director Guy Hamilton told me: "For filming, speak as quickly as you can and act as slowly as you can."

I have never really known what that means. But I know it's good. "Speak as quickly as you can" is the one bit he did explain. "I never know until I'm editing," he said, "how fast

141

a scene should go. If you've spoken quickly I can slow it down, if I want to, with reaction shots and pauses. If you've spoken slowly, I can't speed it up."

I *think*, by "act as slowly as you can" he meant, don't jerk, don't move about too much. But I'm not sure!

He also said, "Save up your reactions until just before you speak. I shall probably cut to you, when I'm editing, for your speeches. Probably. Not always, of course. But as often as not. So save up any acting you want to do until just before you speak. It would be a waste if it ended up on the cutting-room floor."

Radio ⟋

"'You must see with your ears': that is the note I give most often to actors," said David Spenser, one of the best directors of radio drama. "And I say, 'try to convince the microphone that you are looking at the other people, or *not* looking at them; or that you are calling after them, or talking to them on the telephone, or talking to them while you are doing something else, like looking through a microscope or reading a book; and you should be able to do all these things without looking up from the script. You must see, you must look, with your ears.'"

"Quite hard," I said.

"Yes, it is," he said.

"Demands a lot of observation, a sort of aural observation, I suppose?"

"Yes," he said. We were talking on the telephone. "But you see, what I'm using now is a telephone voice. I know that to talk on the telephone is different from talking outside, or in a car, or to the cast of a radio play. Yes. A good radio actor will know all these differences. And he will also know how to ignore punctuation, so that the thought-line matters more than the sentences."

"Oh yes," I said, "good. Of course, when you've learnt the lines for the theatre or television you forget about punctuation altogether, but there it is, staring the radio actor in the face."

"That's right," he said.

"Anything else?" I said, for my own benefit really, for I'm not an experienced radio actor.

"Oh, just, oh, play the microphone. The microphone is your audience, and it's an audience of one. You don't have to project. As long as your thoughts are accurate, the microphone will accept them."

Commentaries And Voice-Overs ⌣

Commentaries for films and voice-overs for commercials: delightful jobs, both, delightful perks, both. And they both rely on your having a sort of microphone-presence—a good forward voice, a voice with an edge to it—and on your diligence in acquiring certain knacks.

As far as I understand it, the knacks are these:

1. Keep as steady a level of volume as you can, even trying to make the ends of words no quieter than the beginnings. This is harder than it sounds. You know when you hear a tape played backwards and it sounds like Russian? That is because in Russian words get louder as they progress, whereas in English they tend to get quieter. Say "Quieter". "Qui" is louder than "er". The more you can level it up the more the microphone likes it.

2. Keep a steady tone. Don't change gear.

3. Don't breathe audibly. The microphone doesn't like those sudden, rushed intakes of breath. Hard to avoid sometimes, when one long sentence is immediately followed

by another, but a huge breath just before you start will help.

4. Develop an acute sense of timing, coming in immediately that cue-line has whizzed across the screen or immediately "the pack-shot" (the final close-up of the product being advertised) comes up at the end.

"Brutal soap. The soap you can trust."

It's nice if the B of Brutal coincides with the cut to the pack-shot.

5. Be obedient. They have worked for months on their film, and you are the last arrival. They have fought and argued over every shot and every word. They know more or less exactly how they would like you to sound. If they tell you, be obedient. But ...

6. ... be sincere. It is important to believe, for the moment of doing it, that Brutal soap really is the soap you can trust.

7. Be quick. For a usual fifteen- thirty- or sixty-second commercial you will not normally have had a previous sight of the script, and the recording-studio will have been booked for only half-an-hour or an hour. It is important to be quick at grasping what is required, and to use the utmost concentration. You can help yourself achieve this, and make fluffing less likely, by reading something aloud, at sight, for fifteen minutes at home before you go. It will put you into a good reading mood.

Voice And Concentration ⌒·

It is worth doing similar exercises at home before you go to the theatre for your performance, for you will enjoy yourself much more and feel much better if you are "in voice" (in the singer's sense) and in a good concentrating mood.

One's bad nights—regrettably more numerous than one would like—are often due to being out of voice (husky, throaty, quiet) and being unable to concentrate.

Bad Nights ⌣

Wendy Hiller calls these bad nights No Man's Land. "Darling, I'm in No Man's Land," she would wail. "I don't know who I am, where I am, or what I'm doing."

There are always nights like this in a long run. And you just have to say to yourself, well... it'll be better tomorrow...

If it's not, then a little homework might help, especially if it yields a new idea, something you have never put into the part before. It's like having a new picture or ornament at home. It makes you look at the pictures and ornaments you already have all over again, and makes you realise how long it is since you looked at them properly.

A good wheeze is to pretend that the next performance after a bad night is not a performance at all but a rehearsal. "Pretend the tabs are down," said Murray Macdonald, "and there's no audience there."

Wendy Hiller and I used to say to each other, when one of us had been in No Man's Land the previous evening: "Let's do it for each other. Not for the audience. You talk to me and listen to me, and I'll talk to you and listen to you." We both found this an enormously helpful corrective, for it pointed out to us just how much we had been forgetting each other, and merely addressing the audience and listening to their coughs and sneezes.

But don't forget that whereas you are comparing your performance with your previous ones, the audience is not. It won't be nearly as bad, or as different, as you think.

You And The Audience ⌒

Nevertheless, there will be those nights when you feel the audience is decidedly hostile towards you. Towards you personally. "They hate me tonight": I think I must have heard every actor I have acted with say that at some time or other. I have certainly said it often enough myself. "They cough in my quiet bits and I just cannot get the laughs I am used to. It's all right for the rest of you, it's me they hate."

It can be very demoralising; confidence can sink to a surprisingly low level and self-consciousness set in. Of course the changes to the performance are minimal, but they hurt. What I have noticed is that, when confidence goes, attack goes too. And speed. So a good way to get the audience back on your side is to go a little louder and a little faster. "Down" nights are quiet, and slow, nights.

Laughs In The Wrong Place ⌒·

One of the most unpleasant things that can happen to an actor is to get titters in the wrong place. You are being derided in public and it is terribly dispiriting. It can happen in modern plays when the dialogue is of questionable quality, but it can more easily happen in plays of a few decades ago: those by Wilde, Shaw, Ibsen, Galsworthy and others. The serious bits in *A Woman of No Importance*, for example, can present an unconvinced audience with a field-day, so mawkish are the sentiments the poor actors have to deliver.

Besides bringing the utmost sincerity and clarity of intention and attitude to such awkward passages, there are a number of remedies you can try, and they are all, really, the opposite of some of the ideas for comedy which I outlined earlier.

So: *Do* fade out at the ends of sentences.
Don't keep the rhythm of the lines: split them up and *don't* do slack turns of the head.

In particular, fading out at the ends of sentences is a good antidote: it makes that possibly funny line sound much more serious; a melancholy fills the air, and the audience will probably be stilled.

151

Good Nights ✎

On your good nights everything (as that other soap commercial says) feels "fresh and alive", and you feel especially pleased with yourself when this happens after the play has been running for a long time. "I'm still capable of spontaneity, even after all these months," you think.

You can help yourself to these good nights, and give your performance a wash-and-brush-up, by telling yourself little stories before you go on, like:

1. Pretend the play is by somebody else. If it's by Alan Ayckbourn pretend it's by Chekhov.
2. Pretend, if it's a comedy, it's a serious play.
3. Pretend, if it's a serious play, it's a comedy.
4. Pretend you are another actor playing your part.
5. Pretend it has never been written down, and that you are improvising it.

These secret games are amusing to play and, don't worry, they won't alter your performance much: they will just freshen it up.

Giggling ⌒

I used to be a dreadful giggler, and am still capable of it, as the cast of *Donkeys' Years* knew only too well. I'm not as bad as I used to be because I'm more nervous now, but it is a terrible affliction, and of course it can ruin a play for the audience.

I remember two dreadful nights in *Crown Matrimonial* at the Haymarket Theatre.

Half-way through a very tense scene, Wendy Hiller, Amanda Reiss and I noticed that Andrew Ray's stiff white collar had come away from his shirt, for the stud had broken and flown off with a ping. We managed to keep going but saw to our horror that his collar started rising up his neck until it covered his chin. He then had to say: "All this passion is very fine. But what is happening now?"

I was supposed to be the next to speak, but couldn't because all I could think of as a reply was, "Your collar's come undone."

And in the last scene of the play, a duologue between Queen Mary and David, the Duke of Windsor, there was this exchange:

QUEEN: As to the question of a job, what job? You refused Bermuda.

DAVID: Whose macabre idea was that? I cannot agree to be shunted from remote island to remote island. It's a wonder I wasn't offered St Helena.

QUEEN: Bermuda would have accepted you. Nowhere else will...

One night I just couldn't remember St Helena. The only island I could think of quickly was the Isle of Wight. So I said it. Wendy Hiller paused for what seemed like an eternity, then decided to say "The Isle of Wight would have accepted you. Nowhere else will."

I don't know how we finished the scene.

The best remedy I know is to say to yourself: "All right, go ahead and laugh, you fool ... go on ... show the audience you are laughing." It's the most relaxing antidote there is—giving yourself permission to laugh if you want to—and it sometimes works.

Mistakes ⌣

I like the old actors' adage: If you make a mistake, acknowledge it. It is no use pretending it hasn't happened.

If you trip over a rug, acknowledge it. Look at the rug. Straighten it.

If ash drops on a carpet, acknowledge it, and do something about it.

If you drop a glass and it breaks, pick up the pieces. If your cigarette goes out, re-light it.

Of course, if you are recording a television play, you'll get a re-take!

A Happy Company ·∽·

A happy company is essential, and anything you can do to prevent unhappiness and induce happiness will be worth it. As I have said before in this book, it is impossible to concentrate in an unfriendly atmosphere. Nip any kind of crossness in the bud, and keep a sense of humour to the fore.

A happy company is based in generosity. And generosity on the stage consists of not upstaging your colleagues any more than you have to, of downstaging yourself whenever you possibly can, of not distracting when the focus of attention should be on someone else, and of really listening. I suppose the general rule is that you can move about as much as you want to when it's your turn, but you should remain as still as you can (without freezing) when it's someone else's. If you move about the audience will look at you. So if you move about, say, in the pause between a feed-line and someone else's laugh-line, you can bet your bottom dollar their laugh will be diminished, and they will not thank you for it. Actors become very sensitive to laughs in a long run, and one of the main causes of argument and, possibly, friction, is the loss of a laugh on account of what someone else is doing.

"Acting is like tennis," said Edith Evans. "We hit the ball to each other and the audience follows the ball. Now it's your turn, now it's mine. And when it's my turn you must not distract. You must just listen to me. And try to listen to me as though for the first time. Never forget, you do not know what I am going to say, right up to my last syllable. You must not anticipate what I am going to say."

Tennis. Yes. Now it's your turn, now it's mine. That helps keep a company happy. And it helps keep the audience happy, too, for they know where to look.

Do Your Best ❧

This was one of the last things my dear old friend Edith
Evans said to me. *The Chinese Prime Minister* was coming to an
end and I had no job to go to. "Don't worry," she said. "Just
do your best. That's all you can do. If you do your best, good
things will come."

She meant, of course, do your best at every rehearsal, at
every performance (including the matinées), and in everyday
life as well: at dinner-parties, at meetings, whenever you are
with people.

Speak The Speech ◆⌐•

I said right at the beginning of this book that I liked to start classes at RADA with that quotation from Stanislavsky.

I always used to end the last lesson with every class by reciting a speech which the students knew only too well, Hamlet's advice to the players, for I had used it for many an exercise during their course; but it is full of gold, and so I'll end this book with it too.

"Speak the speech, I pray you, as I pronounc'd it to you, trippingly on the tongue; but if you mouth it, as many of our players do, I had as lief the town-crier spoke my lines. Nor do not saw the air too much with your hand, thus, but use all gently; for in the very torrent, tempest, and, as I may say, whirlwind of your passion, you must acquire and beget a temperance that may give it smoothness. O, it offends me to the soul to hear a robustious periwig-pated fellow tear a passion to tatters, to very rags, to split the ears of the groundlings, who, for the most part, are capable of nothing but inexplicable dumb shows and noise. I would have such a fellow whipp'd for o'erdoing Termagant; it

159

out-herods Herod. Pray you avoid it.

"Be not too tame neither, but let your own discretion be your tutor. Suit the action to the word, the word to the action; with this special observance, that you o'erstep not the modesty of nature; for anything so o'erdone is from the purpose of playing, whose end, both at the first and now, was and is to hold, as 'twere, the mirror up to nature; to show virtue her own feature, scorn her own image, and the very age and body of the time his form and pressure. Now, this overdone or come tardy off, though it makes the unskilful laugh, cannot but make the judicious grieve, the censure of the which one must, in your allowance, o'erweigh a whole theatre of others. O, there be players that I have seen play—and heard others praise, and that highly—not to speak it profanely, that, neither having th' accent of Christians, nor the gait of Christian, pagan, nor man, have so strutted and bellowed that I have thought some of Nature's journeymen had made men, and not made them well, they imitated humanity so abominably.

"O, reform it altogether. And let those that play your clowns speak no more than is set down for them; for there be of them that will themselves laugh, to set on some quantity of barren spectators to laugh too, though in the meantime some necessary question of the play be then to be considered. That's villainous, and shows a most pitiful ambition in the fool that uses it. Go, make you ready."